THE BBC MICRO REVEALED

Jeremy Ruston

Published by INTERFACE

INTRODUCTION

There are some difficult, but rewarding, hours ahead of you now that you've bought this book.

I hope that by the time you've finished reading it you'll know a great deal more about your computer than you do at the moment, and will have gained a degree of skill to improve your programming.

Although I've made certain assumptions as to things you already know — such as how to use ? (PEEK and POKE) and ! — nearly all of the book is self-explanatory, so long as you read it carefully in the order in which it is presented, and so long as you enter and run the 50 or so programs given. So, even if you're a bit hazy as to the meaning of terms such as "byte" or "register", you'll find you should be able to follow the discussions and understand the conclusions I reach.

Don't worry, it's not really that difficult overall, even though some sections may be more difficult to understand than others. You'll need a computer with 32K on board (model A or B) to get the most out of the book, but apart from that, all the facilities you need are in your hands.

Jeremy Ruston,
London, 1982.

Published in Great Britain by:

INTERFACE,
44–46 Earls Court Road,
LONDON W8 6EJ.

ISBN 0 907563 15 5

Copyright   J Ruston, 1982.
First printing June, 1982.
Second printing November, 1982.
Third printing January, 1983.

Any enquiries regarding the contents of this book should be directed by mail to the above address.

This book is dedicated to Philip and Penny O'Rorke, Nick Ruston, Annabelle Ruston, Emma Lydon-Stanford, Juliet Horsman, Arabella Stuart, Sue Cammack, Neda Said and the inmates of Sheriff House, Rugby School.

PRINTED BY J W DUNN (PRINTERS) LTD · CHEAM · SURREY

Section one: the 6845 CRTC

The television section of the BBC micro is based around a special chip, the 6845, running in conjunction with the ULA. There are other bits and bobs, but we are not concerned with them for the moment. Both of these chips rival the 6502 as far as complexity is concerned, but the 6845 is considerably easier to use. This chapter describes the hardware used, and how to program the 6845 yourself.

By necessity, the hardware section which follows is complex. It is not essential to the rest of the book, but shows some of the lines of thought pursued by Acorn when they were designing the BBC computer, and so merits your attention.

Before discussing the Beeb way of doing things, it is important that you understand how the video section of a typical, old fashioned, micro works. The following account is based on the old PET's video section.

An area of 1000 bytes of memory is used by both the computer and the video circuitry. To the computer this area appears as a normal block of memory, starting at address 32768 and continuing to 33767, assuming the screen format is 25 lines of 40 characters. The video circuitry translates the data stored in the memory to the pictures you see on the screen. It does so by accessing each character position of the block in turn, and then displaying the correct character at the correct point on the screen. A description follows the circuit diagram.

Simplified 'PET' VDU circuitry

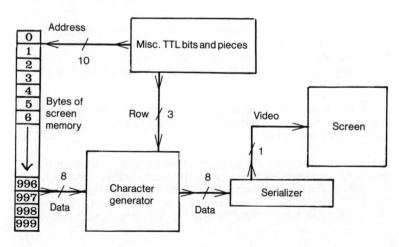

5

This circuit is simplified — some of the important points and features have been left out. Each character on the PET screen is made up out of an 8 by 8 matrix, the same as the BBC micro in modes 0 to 6. Thus, there are 64 bits needed to make up each character. These bits are stored in the 'character generator' like this:

ADDRESS	BINARY DATA
0000	00000000
0001	00111100
0002	00100100
0003	00100100
0004	00100100
0005	00100100
0006	00111100
0007	00000000

And so on with the rest of the characters. The character shown above is a 'box' shape. As you can see, eight bytes of storage are required for each character. The type of ROM used for a character generator can hold 2048 bytes, which means that its address bus is 11 bits wide. If you divide 2048 by eight you get 256, which is the total number of displayable characters on the PET screen. 256 characters need eight bits to be represented uniquely. So, the 11 address lines of the character generator are used as follows:

Low order 3 bits — character row (0 to 7)
High order 8 bits — character select (0 to 255)

So to access the data stored in the 5th row of the 45th character, we need to put the following data on the character generator's address lines:

A0 to A2 — 5
A3 to A10 — 45.

You can see the 11 lines going in to the character generator in the diagram. The data bus of the character generator is connected to a serializer, which is a simple chip which accepts eight bits, and then clocks the bits out at a pre-determined rate, one at a time. This chip is typically a 74165.

Thus, to display the fifth row of the 45th character, the above procedure should be carried out, and the required byte will be clocked to the TV by the serializer.

You can also see from the diagram where the eight 'character select' inputs to the character generator come from — they are simply the contents of the memory location currently being accessed in the VDU RAM. The 'row select' signal comes from the TTL bits and pieces. These pieces access the VDU RAM at the right time, with the right row

6

output to the character generator, eight times, once for each row of each character.

The point of that explanation was to show you how the character generator works. This arrangement is similar to that used in the teletext mode of the BBC computer, except a special character generator is used, the SA5050, and the matrix for each character is much larger, 16 by 16.

The other modes are dot resolution modes. Before discussing these modes, we have to make another comparison, this time with the Atom. The Atom's highest resolution screen is mapped like this, with reference to the start of VDU RAM, which is again 32768:

Atom high resolution screen mapping

0	1	2	3	———————→	29	30	31
32	33	34	35	———————→	61	62	63
64	—	—→		———————→	—	—→	
96	—	—→		———————→	—	—→	
128	—	—→		———————→	—	—→	

etc...

Contrast this to the BBC's arrangement:

The Beeb's mode 4 RAM arrangement

0	8	⟶	312
1	9	⟶	313
2	10	⟶	314
3	11	⟶	315
4	12	⟶	316
5	13	⟶	317
6	14	⟶	318
7	15	⟶	319
320	328	⟶	632
321	329	⟶	633
322	330	⟶	634
323	331	⟶	635
324	332	⟶	636
325	333	⟶	637
326	334	⟶	638
327	335	⟶	639

ETC

N.B. The shaded portion shows where the first character on the screen will lie.

It looks a little odd compared to the Atom arrangement, but we shall see that it is logical.

To put off the moment when we have to start on the rest of the hardware, here are the details of how the individual bits map on to the display.

In all modes with two possible colours, the arrangement is as follows:

Pixels:	p0	p1	p2	p3	p4	p5	p6	p7
Bits:	b7	b6	b5	b4	b3	b2	b1	b0

In this table, p0 is the leftmost pixel of a group of eight, and b0 is the low order bit. Therefore, a byte with 128 in it will appear as 'X0000000', where an 'X' represents a white spot, and 'O' represents a black spot.

In modes with 4 colours, each byte only accounts for four pixels. The arrangement is like this:

Pixel:	p0	p1	p2	p3
Bits:	b0/b4	b1/b5	b2/b6	b3/b7

This arrangement is a bit odd, but will only really concern the machine code programmer.

Mode 2 is mapped like this:

Pixels:	p0	p1
Bits:	b0/b2/b4/b6	b1/b3/b5/b7

The best way of experimenting to see these arrangements is to move to the required mode, press 'return' a few times and then type CLG. The top left of the screen will now be blank. You can put any byte you like into the top left position using '?H. = X', ('H.' is the abbreviation for HIMEM). When doing this, do not scroll the screen.

Back to the BBC computer's circuits:

I have chosen mode 4 as an example, but all modes work roughly the same, except mode 7.

The 6845 is a clever piece of equipment, which basically acts as the TTL bits and pieces in the PET. There are some more sophisticated things it can do. It generates the cursor, scrolls the screen and deals with the light pen.

Take a look at the circuit diagram:

Simplified BBC Mode 4. VDU circuitry

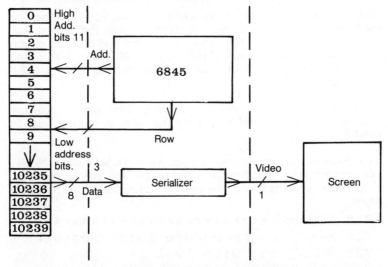

(Dotted lines indicate approximate position of ULA.)

The first important point to note is the absence of a character generator. The second difference between this diagram and the first is that the PET VDU takes 1000 bytes of RAM, but the BBC computer takes a vast 10K to generate a picture.

The same process is carried out to generate a picture as on the PET, except that the character generator row address makes up the lowest three bits of the VDU RAM address. Thus, rather than the code for a particular character being held in VDU RAM, the dot pattern for the entire character is held, byte by byte in VDU RAM.

Each VDU RAM location is only accessed once, but if you forget about the low order three bits for a moment, each group of eight VDU RAM locations is accessed eight times, once for each row of each character.

In the case of graphics, because each screen location is in effect its own character generator, VDU RAM can be written bit (as in byte) by bit.

The rôle of the ULA is to deal with the scrolling mechanism, the colours, and the addressing mechanism, because the character generator is only used in mode 7.

All communications between you and the 6845 are carried out via 18 'ports'. These ports are like variables, except that some may only be written to, and some others may only be read and two can be both written to and read from. These ports are referred to as 'registers'.

There are two ways to get a number into a register. You can either use the command 'VDU 23, 0, reg, val, 0;0;0;' to copy the number 'val' into register number 'reg' (the registers are numbered 0 to 17), or you can execute the statements '?&FE00 = reg: ?&FE01 = val'. The second way is usually best to use in machine language, and the first is the neater way in BASIC.

There is only one way to read the number held in a register. Execute '?&FE00 = reg: val = ?&FE01' to copy the value in register 'reg' to variable 'val'.

If you have your machine turned on, you will find it helpful to enter the following procedure and function, used to read and write to registers, so you can experiment with the registers discussed in the next few pages.

```
 900 REM ******************************
 910 REM This procedure loads register
 920 REM 'reg' with 'val'.
 930 REM ******************************
1000 DEF PROCLOAD(reg,val)
```

```
1010 VDU 23,0,reg,val,0,0,0,0,0,0
1020 ENDPROC
1030 REM ******************************
1910 REM This function returns the
1920 REM value in register 'reg'.
1930 REM ******************************
2000 DEF FNREAD(reg)
2010 ?&FE00=reg
2020=?&FE01
2030 REM ******************************
```

There follows a description of each of the 18 registers.

The first few registers are not very interesting, in that altering them serves no useful purpose, except sometimes collapsing your display, so I'll skate over them quickly.

Register 0 — 'Horizontal total'. (Write only).

The contents of this register determine the total time allocated to each scan line in terms of character clocks. In other words it contains the total number of displayed and undisplayed characters on the screen, minus one, per horizontal line. Thus it determines the horizontal SYNC frequency. Its contents in the various modes are as follows:

Mode —	0	1	2	3	4	5	6	7
Contents —	127	127	127	127	63	63	63	63

The numbers are larger than the number of characters per line, to allow for a border. This leads on to an important point, namely that from the above table, it looks as though modes 0 to 3 have the same number of characters, as do modes 4 to 7. This is in fact so.

It transpires that modes 0 to 3 have 80 characters to a line, and the others have 40. The reason why modes 1,2, and 5 do not appear to have the right number of characters per line is that they allow more than two colours. The range of values for register 0 is 0 to 255.

Register 1 — 'Characters per line.' (Write only).

This register determines the number of characters to be displayed on each horizontal line. This register is loaded with the number of characters actually displayed per line. Thus, the difference between this register and register Ø are the borders on the sides of the display.

The contents of this register in each of the modes are as follows:

Mode —	Ø	1	2	3	4	5	6	7
Contents —	80	80	80	80	40	40	40	40

This table reinforces the comments I made about the number of characters per line in the discussion of register Ø.

You can put anything you like in this register and see the effect, but if you make the contents of this register larger than the contents of register Ø, the display collapses. This is because the border will be a negative number of characters, which confuses the 6845.

If you just increment or decrement this register from its normal value, you get a slanted display, which can be quite dramatic. This program uses register 1 in a number of ways.

```
10 MODE 5
20 VDU 19,3,4,0,0,0,19,0,7,0,0,0,19,
   2,0,0,0,0
30 FOR T=0 TO 14
40 COLOUR RND(3)
50 PRINT "Interface..."'
60 NEXT T
61 TIME=0
62 REPEAT UNTIL TIME>100
70 TIME=0
80 REPEAT
90 FOR T=1 TO 40
100 PROCLOAD(1,T)
110 G=TIME
120 REPEAT UNTIL (TIME-G)>20
130 NEXT T
135 G=TIME
136 REPEAT UNTIL (TIME-G)>50
140 FOR T=39 TO 2 STEP -1
```

```
150 PROCLOAD(1,T)
160 G=TIME
170 REPEAT UNTIL (TIME-G)>20
180 NEXT T
190 UNTIL TIME>1000
200 TIME=0
210 REPEAT UNTIL TIME>100
220 MODE 2
230 PROCLOAD(1,79)
240 TIME=0
250 REPEAT
260 COLOUR RND(7)
270 VDU 8,8,42
280 UNTIL TIME>1000
290 REPEAT UNTIL FALSE
999 REM *****************************
1000 DEF PROCLOAD(reg,val)
1010 VDU 23,0,reg,val,0,0,0,0,0,0
1020 ENDPROC
2000 DEF FNREAD(reg)
2010 ?&FE00=reg
2020=?&FE01
```

The range of values for register 1 is 0 to 255 — but more realistically the upper limit is the contents of register 0.

Register 2 — 'Horizontal SYNC position'. (Write only).

This register establishes the point where the horizontal SYNC signal switches. It is specified in terms of characters. The reference point is the left most character position displayed on the screen.

What this means is that this register determines the displacement from the left-hand side of the screen of the left most character in the display. The contents of this register in each of the 8 modes are as follows:

Mode —	0	1	2	3	4	5	6	7
Contents —	98	98	98	98	49	49	49	51

If you increase the number given in the above table the whole display will move to the left, if you decrease it, the display moves to the right. Some characters may be lost at the edges of the screen. Altering the value by more than a few characters collapses the display.

The range for this register is 0 to 255.

Register 3 — 'Horizontal SYNC width'. (Write only).

This register establishes the duration of the horizontal SYNC pulse. *DO NOT ADJUST IT!!!*

Register 4 — 'Vertical total'. (Write only).

This register gives the total number of displayed and undisplayed character rows, or lines. The contents of this register in the 8 modes are as follows:

Mode —	0	1	2	3	4	5	6	7
Contents —	38	38	38	30	38	38	30	30

As a consequence of its function, this register helps determine the frame refresh rate, 50 Hz. Thus, if you alter its value too radically, you're likely to lose synchronisation.

There is little point in altering this register, except that if you reduce its value by about 1 or 2, it is possible to move the display up the screen a bit.

The range of this register is 0 to 127.

Register 5 — 'Vertical SYNC adjust'. (Write only).

It was stated above that register 4 helps determine the frame refresh rate. Register 4 is a coarse adjustment, while register 5 enables more accurate, fine, adjustments to be made. Zero is usually stored in this register, except mode 7, where 2 is stored.

If you alter its value, you can move the vertical position of the display a little, but numbers should be kept fairly low — some televisions are not very tolerant of differences in the SYNC pulse, and so may cause the picture to collapse.

The range of register 5 is 0 to 31.

Register 6 — 'Character rows per frame'. (Write only).

This register allows you to alter the number of lines displayed on the screen. There are, however, some severe limitations. In mode 7, altering the number of lines causes characters to be sliced up, and in other modes, increasing the number of lines beyond the normal will lead to repetitions, ie some lines appear twice! Also, the height of the lines is not affected, so if you ask the computer to display 40 lines in mode 0, it will, but six of them will probably be off the display. Reducing the number of lines is quite possible.

The range of this register is 0 to 127.

Register 7 — 'Vertical SYNC position'. (Write only).

This register normally contains the number of lines on the screen, plus three.

Altering this register gives you another way of moving the picture up and down the screen. Increasing it from its normal value moves the display up, and decreasing it moves the display down. A similar function is performed by the *TV MOS command.

The range of this register is 0 to 127.

Register 8 — 'Interlace mode'. (Write only).

This register holds a number between 0 and 3 inclusive. The effects of the numbers are as follows:

0 — Non-interlaced picture
1 — Interlaced SYNC picture
2 — Non-interlaced picture
3 — Interlaced SYNC and VIDEO picture

Mode 7 is interlaced with SYNC and VIDEO. All other modes are just interlaced SYNC.

Interlaced pictures are more complete than non-interlaced pictures — if you turn off interlace (which you can't do in mode 7) the lines that make up characters become visible.

There is little point in altering this register. If you do want to, you are better off using *TV with a second argument, as described in the User Guide.

Register 9 — 'Scan lines per row'. (Write only).

The contents of this register determine the total number of vertical dots that go to make up each character. Its contents in each mode are as follows:

Mode —	0	1	2	3	4	5	6	7
Contents —	7	7	7	9	7	7	9	18

In fact, the number loaded is one *less* than the total, so the numbers above tell us that there are eight vertical dots to characters in modes 0,1,2,4 and 5, which we knew already from our knowledge of the VDU 23 command for redefining characters 224 to 255. It also tells us that in modes 3 and 6, two extra lines are inserted, to give the spacing between lines.

You can see the size of the mode 7 matrix from the last value in the table.

Register 10 — 'Cursor start line'. (Write only).

Each character on the display stretches over a number of 'scan lines'. The exact number for each mode is given in the section on register 9. The cursor can extend between any two of these scan lines. In mode 7, for example, the cursor starts and stops on the last scan line of the character, giving the impression of a single bar, but in modes 3 and 6 it starts on scan line 7, and finishes on scan line 9, which is why the cursor appears thicker in these modes.

The contents of this register determine the first scan line on which the cursor will appear. Thus, its contents in each of the 8 modes are as follows:

Mode —	0	1	2	3	4	5	6	7
Contents —	7	7	7	7	7	7	7	18

In fact, the register does not contain these numbers on their own. However, register 10 does contain numbers combined with information about the flash rate of the cursor, and whether it is visible or not. Add these numbers for the following attributes for the cursor:

Number to be added	Attribute
0	Cursor doesn't blink
32	Cursor invisible
64	Cursor flashes quickly
96	Cursor flashes slowly

The cursor normally flashes slowly, so the actual values stored for each mode are as follows:

Mode —	0	1	2	3	4	5	6	7
Contents —	103	103	103	103	103	103	103	114
	(96 + 7)	(96 + 7)	(96 + 7)	(96 + 7)	(96 + 7)	(96 + 7)	(96 + 7)	(96 + 18)

If you execute 'VDU 23,0,10,64,0;0;0;', to make the cursor blink quickly and start at the first scan line, in mode 7, you will be amazed to see that if you type control-K a few times (so that the cursor is over some character already on the screen) reverse field characters can be displayed. Altering the above 64 to zero would give a solid, unblinking, cursor, which would show the effect better. It is normally impossible to display reverse video in this way in mode 7.

One application of this register is to alter the cursor's appearance in a program to show which mode you're in (I don't mean *screen* mode). I will give some examples of cursors after the discussion of the next register. The range of the first part of this register is 0 to 31.

Register 11 — 'Cursor stop line'. (Write only).

This register gives the last scan line on which the cursor will appear. Its contents in all the modes are as follows:

Mode —	0	1	2	3	4	5	6	7
Contents —	7	7	7	9	7	7	9	19

(This table gives the impression that the mode 7 cursor is two scan lines deep — it is, but because of the way the SA5050 character generator operates, only one scan line appears to be used).

All of the following examples are to be tried in any mode *but* mode 7.

Start scan line	Stop scan line	Effect
0	0	Underlines the character *above* the cursor
4	4	Gives a narrow, centralized, dash cursor
3	6	Gives a thick dash as a cursor
4	7	Gives a cursor occupying half the space allocated to it.

You can probably quite easily make up your own cursors — but remember, contrary to popular belief, you cannot make the cursor any ASCII character you want.

Registers 12 & 13 — 'Top of page'. (Write only). MSB LSB

These two registers behave differently in modes 0 to 6 from mode 7. I'll discuss them first in modes 0 to 6, then go on to talk about mode 7.

MODES 0 TO 6:

In these modes, registers 12 and 13 indicate the lowest memory address that is being used by the current screen mode. For this purpose the least significant byte of the address is stored in register 13, and the most significant is stored in register 12. However, you don't store the actual address in these registers — you have to use the address divided by 8. So this procedure will, in combination with the one you've already got in memory, make the current screen mode start at any address you choose:

```
  30 REM This procedure makes
  40 REM VDU RAM at any address
  50 REM (modes 0 to 6 only)
 800 DEF PROCSTART(address)
 805 address=address DIV 8
 810 PROCLOAD(12,address DIV 256)
 820 PROCLOAD(13,address MOD 256)
 830 ENDPROC
 999 REM ******************************
1000 DEF PROCLOAD(reg,val)
1010 VDU 23,0,reg,val,0,0,0,0,0,0
1020 ENDPROC
2000 DEF FNREAD(reg)
2010 ?&FE00=reg
2020=?&FE01
```

One interesting thing you can do with this procedure is to set the display to start at address 0. If you do, you can see all the lower memory locations being changed very rapidly. Run through the following examples:

Execute MODE 0/VDU 28,0,10,79,0/PROCSTART(0) to put you in mode 0, with screen memory starting at address 0. The VDU 28 command defines a text window which keeps the cursor in the visible part of the screen. (MODE 0 takes up 20K, if you make it start at

25

address Ø the screen will overlap with the old mode Ø — ie you can see what you type, which you can't do if you do all this in mode 4.) The screen should look something like this:

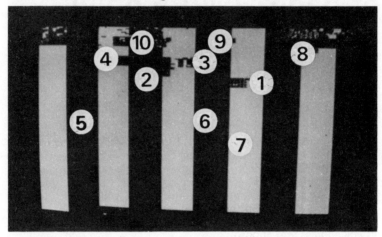

1. PROGRAM   2. KEYS   3. SOUND QUEUE   4. ENVELOPES
5. CHARS 64-95   6. CHARS 32-64   7. CHARS 96-127
8. KEYBOARD BUFFER   9. RUN TIME BUFFER   10. COPY

I have annotated the diagram to show where various things are stored. Try the following, and watch the relevant areas of the screen as you do so. Insert some extra lines (REM statements, perhaps) in your program. You will see the area labelled 'PROGRAM' expand. If you then delete some lines, you can see the same area contracting, as less memory is used up.

Execute 'FOR T% = TOP TO HIMEM:? T% = Ø:NEXT'. This will clear the unused area of memory.

Define a user defined key. The area labelled 'KEYS' will expand slightly.

Type a SOUND statement and you will see the 'SOUND QUEUE' area become active. Similarly, type an ENVELOPE, and you will see the ENVELOPE storage area, labelled 'ENVELOPES', pop into life.

Try redefining the letter 'A', using VDU 23,65,1,2,3,4,5,6,7,8. The area labelled 'CHARS 64 TO 95' will get filled with the dot patterns of the aforementioned characters.

Similarly defining any character will bring that labelled area of memory into life. If you've got a long program in memory, though, you are likely to overwrite it — so be careful!

Watch the area labelled 'KEYBOARD BUFFER' as you type text in at the keyboard.

Then execute a loop such as 'TIME = 0:REPEAT UNTIL TIME = 10*100'. While the loop is executing, watch the area labelled 'RUN TIME BUFFER' as you type text in. When the loop has finished, the 'KEYBOARD BUFFER' will get filled up.

Watch the area called 'COPY' when you use the copy key to copy characters. If you are a little confused at this stage, no need to worry as all the things you are watching will be explained in subsequent chapters.

Back now to more serious matters:

If you make screen memory start at an address before its normal address (ie lower than HIMEM), you will see that only a part of the normal screen will be shown, if any, but if you make the start address larger than normal, the screen 'wraps around'. This means that instead of starting to display characters above the place where memory should stop, it goes back to the start of official screen RAM, and displays that instead. This is how the scrolling of memory is done so fast on the computer — it doesn't have to alter anything to scroll the screen, except these registers.

This program uses the scrolling principle outlined above to print in mode 4, and then allows you to 'roll' the screen in any direction, using the cursor control keys.

Just type RUN, then manipulate the cursor keys. Various games using this principle spring to mind. (INKEY is used with a negative argument, so you can press combinations of keys for diagonal movement).

```
  10 REM Movement
  20 REM For modes 4 and 5.
  30 REM Modes 0,1 & 2 - see below.
  40 REM (C) 1982 Jeremy Ruston.
  50 REM ************************
  60 MODE 4
  70 PRINT TAB(7,16);"The BBC Micro Rev
ealed..."
  80 PROCASSEMBLE
  90 START=HIMEM/8
 100 X=0
 110 Y=0
 120 REM ************************
 130 REPEAT
 140 IF INKEY(-42) THEN Y=(Y+31) MOD 32
```

```
150 IF INKEY(-58) THEN Y=(Y+1) MOD 32
160 IF INKEY(-26) THEN X=(X+1) MOD 40
170 IF INKEY(-122) THEN X=(X+39) MOD 4
0
180 S=START+X+Y*40
190 ?&D00=S DIV 256
200 ?&D01=S MOD 256
210 CALL &D10
220 UNTIL FALSE
230 REM ************************
240 REM Machine code routine to load
250 REM register 12 with the contents
260 REM of &D00 and 13 with that of
270 REM &D01.  Has to be in MC for
280 REM high speed.
290 DEF PROCASSEMBLE
300 P%=&D10
310[OPT 0
320 LDA #12:STA &FE00
330 LDA &D00:STA &FE01
340 LDA #13:STA &FE00
350 LDA &D01:STA &FE01
360 RTS:]
370 ENDPROC
380 REM ************************
390 For modes 0,1 and 2, make these
400 changes :
410
420 Line 180 becomes :
430 IF INKEY(-26) THEN X=(X+1) MOD 80
440 Line 190 becomes :
450 IF INKEY(-122) THEN X=(X+79) MOD 8
0
460 Line 200 becomes :
470 S=START+X+Y*80
```

Before scrolling takes place in any of these modes, the value in register 13 is always zero. So you can do a certain amount of work just using register 13 for scrolling from side to side. For example:

```
10 MODE 2
20 VDU 29,640;512;
30 VDU 24,-639;-511;639;511;
40 GCOL 0,132
50 CLG
60 VDU 24,-499;-399;499;399;
70 GCOL 0,128
80 CLG
90 FOR T=1 TO 100
100 X=RND(640)-1
110 Y=RND(512)-1
120 GCOL 0,RND(7)
130 FOR ones=-1 TO 1 STEP 2
140 FOR twos=-1 TO 1 STEP 2
150 MOVE 0,0
160 PLOT 1,ones*X,twos*Y
170 NEXT twos
180 NEXT ones
190 NEXT T
200 DELAY=0
210 FOR T=1 TO 79 STEP 2
220 FOR A=1 TO T
230 PROCLOAD(13,A)
240 PROCDELAY(DELAY)
250 NEXT A
260 FOR A=T-1 TO 2 STEP -1
270 PROCLOAD(13,A)
280 PROCDELAY(DELAY)
290 NEXT A
300 NEXT T
310 PROCLOAD(13,0)
320 END
330 DEF PROCLOAD(reg,val)
340 VDU 23,0,reg,val,0,0,0,0,0,0
350 ENDPROC
360 DEF PROCDELAY(TIM)
370 TIME=0
380 REPEAT UNTIL TIME>TIM
390 ENDPROC
```

Notice that the scrolling from side to side used here is not the same as the rolling you can achieve with register 2, since with register 2 you often lose characters off the edge of the screen. With register 13 you get full wrap around, to stop you losing any characters.

You should now be able to see why these two registers are called 'TOP of page', and not 'Screen memory start'.

MODE 7:

Things work similarly in mode 7 — except that the address loaded does not have to be divided by 8. The complication is that the start of mode 7 is not quite where you would expect it to be — try it and see. Also, if you decrease the top of page value, to below the normal value, you will not move back by a few bytes — you will move forward by 6700 bytes. This is complex and only amounts to making these registers rather trickier to use. Messing about with register 13 is easy in mode 7, however.

Registers 14 & 15 — 'Cursor address'. (Read and write). MSB LSB

These two registers hold the address of the cursor. The address is held as it should be in mode 7, but in all other modes, the address stored is the actual address divided by 8.

Thus, at a CLS or mode change (under program control, to stop the prompt appearing), the address in these two registers is the same as the address in registers 12 & 13.

Registers 16 & 17 — 'Light pen position'. (Read only).
MSB LSB

This register gives the position of the light pen, as an absolute address. In modes 0 to 6 this address is 8 times too small, but in mode 7 you get the actual address. Not having a light pen, I can't give a very helpful description of these two registers. However, it would appear to make more sense to use *FX136, as described in the manual.

That completes the description of the 6845's internal registers.

For completeness, here is a table showing the contents of the various registers in each of the modes:

Mode —	0	1	2	3	4	5	6	7
0 Register	127	127	127	127	63	63	63	63
1	80	80	80	80	40	40	40	40
2	98	98	98	98	49	49	49	51
4	38	38	38	30	38	38	30	30
5	0	0	0	0	0	0	0	2
6	32	32	32	25	32	32	25	25
7	35	35	35	28	35	35	28	28
8	1	1	1	1	1	1	1	3
9	7	7	7	9	7	7	9	18
10	103	103	103	103	103	103	103	114
11	7	7	7	9	7	7	9	19

Notice that, to the 6845, there is no difference between modes 0,1 and 2, nor is there between modes 4 and 5.

Designing your own modes.

To test our understanding of the registers, let's see if we can use them to make up a screen mode to our own specifications. The only way we can do this is by altering the number of lines and number of characters displayed in an existing mode.

I'll work slowly through the way I managed to get a mode of 16 lines of 32 characters, then it would be instructive for you to see if you can go on to make other modes, of different numbers of characters.

Before we start, make sure you've got PROCLOAD defined at the top of memory, say at line 1000, and then type an END statement at about line 500. This will ensure that as we add extra lines to our program, when we execute it, we won't go charging through the procedure definition, which could cause problems.

Our first choice is to choose an existing mode with which to start work. I chose mode 4, since it is slightly bigger than the format we are aiming at. So, the first line of our program is:

10 MODE 4

We're aiming for a mode with 16 lines. At the moment there are 32, so we've got to get rid of 16 of them. Looking back at our tour of 6845 registers, we can see that the relevant one to change is register 6. So by setting the contents of register 6 to 16 we will instruct the 6845 to display 16 lines of characters. To do this, add the following to your program:

20 PROCLOAD(6,16)

Now run the program. The screen will probably give a little kick, and then settle down to look like a normal mode 4 screen. If you execute 'VDU 19,1,0,0,0,0,19,0,7,0,0,0' you will see that this is not the case. Now that you've got a white background, you can see that only the top half of the screen is being used. That's all very well, but it would be nicer if the 16 lines could be spaced out a little, to fill up all the available screen area. We'll do it in the same way as the extra spaces are inserted into modes 3 and 6. To achieve this spacing, we allow for 16 scan lines per line of text, instead of the normal 8. If you look back a few pages, you will see why this line is the one to be added:

40 PROCLOAD(9,15)

This display should now appear spaced out correctly, but there will probably be a good deal of flicker on the screen, and the first line of text will not start at its accustomed place at the top of the screen.

The reason for the display being half way down the screen is that the vertical total register, register 18, has not been informed of the reduction in the number of screen lines, and so is pumping out a vast border at the top of the screen, which shifts everything else on the screen down a few lines. So we update the vertical total register with:

50 PROCLOAD(4,18)

The display should now start at the right place, but you may find that the picture rolls rather a lot. After much experimentation, it transpires that all we have to do to remove the rolling is to adjust the position of the vertical SYNC pulse. Actually the experimentation consisted of looking at the table of register contents under various modes, seeing which registers held some connection with the number of lines displayed and ensuring that all those had been adjusted. Register 7 was the only one which hadn't. From the table, I expected this register to hold two more than the number of screen lines, but I get a steadier picture with 17 in this register. So the line we can finally add is:

60 PROCLOAD(7,17)

We should now have a perfect display of 16 lines of 40 characters. So now all we have to do is remove 8 characters from the end of each line. Before we do so, you may like to add:

70 PROCLOAD(11,15)

which gives an odd cursor.

To adjust the number of characters in the line, we use:

80 PROCLOAD(1,32)

We now have a screen of 16 lines of 32 characters — but the computer is still treating it as a screen of 32 lines of 40 characters, and so printing will not work as you want.

Finally in this section, here is a table of the 6845 registers:

6845 REGISTERS:

Register	Name/function
0	Horizontal total
1	Characters/row
2	HSYNC position
3	HSYNC width
4	Vertical total
5	VSYNC adjust
6	Character rows/frame

7	VSYNC position
8	Interlace mode
9	Scan lines/row
10	Cursor start scan line
11	Cursor stop scan line
12	MSB Start address (top of page)
13	LSB Start address (top of page)
14	MSB Cursor position
15	LSB Cursor position
16	MSB Light pen position
17	LSB Light pen position

Section two: Memory locations

This section is mainly concerned with exploring the area of memory known as 'page three'. This area extends from location &300 to &3FF. It is used for storage by the VDU drivers. Some other locations are discussed where necessary.

This chapter is only directly applicable to OS EPROM/ROM 0.10.
Users of other MOS versions will still find this chapter useful because of the conversion table provided at the back of this book.

Before I started to investigate the uses of each location, I made a list of the sort of information I expected to find:

1) The lowest address used by the current screen mode.
2) The address of the top left-hand corner of the screen, since scrolling will alter this address.
3) The coordinates of the cursor.
4) The size of the current screen mode, in terms of characters per line and lines per page.
5) The graphics resolution of the current mode.
6) The number of available colours in the current mode.
7) Whether the current mode allows graphics as well as text.
8) The text background and foreground colours.
9) The graphics foreground and background colours, and the GCOL modifier.
10) The printer enable flag. (It is worth pointing out that this flag will probably occupy a single bit, and there are 2048 bits in page three. You can see that the task ahead is not easy!)
11) The separate/joined text and graphics cursors flag.
12) The page mode on/off flag.
13) VDU drivers enable/disable flag.
14) Flags for whether to use the character generator in ROM or RAM, for user defined characters.
15) The extent of the graphics window.
16) The current screen mode.
17) The current and last position of the graphics cursor.
18) The extent of the current text window.
19) Whether scrolling should take place over the whole screen, using the 6845, or locally, area by area.
20) The number of bytes scrolled.
21) The actual colour of each logical colour.
22) The edit mode on/off flag.

The following list of memory locations is in numerical order of address, rather than the order in which I found out their uses. Most sections also detail how I discovered the use of each location, information which could be useful to you in the future, as well as interesting in its own right.

I would suggest that you read the chapter on VDU drivers in the Users Guide thoroughly before progressing with this section.

Before we start, I should explain the difference between the two methods of scrolling the screen.

Text is normally scrolled by altering the 6845's registers 12 and 13. This is very quick, but carries the disadvantage of moving VDU RAM around with reference to the first location on the screen. When a text window is in operation, even if it occupies the whole screen, scrolling takes place by copying each location 'backwards'. Again, although this is slow, it doesn't interfere with registers 12 and 13, which can often be extremely useful.

Locations &320 and &321 — Screen memory start. (16 bits). LSB MSB

In the same way as I presented the contents of the 6845 registers under various modes, here are the contents of locations &320 and &321 in each mode:

Mode —	0	1	2	3	4	5	6	7
Contents —	12288	12288	12288	16384	22528	22528	24576	31744

These values should be instantly recognizable as the value of HIMEM in each of the modes. So it would be safe to assume that this location contains the lowest memory address used for the current screen mode. But look at the program I used to get these values:

```
 10 DIM A%(255,7)
 20 FOR T%=0 TO 7
 30 MODE T%
 40 VDU 28,1,20,17,3
 50 VDU 24,60;50;532;432;
 60 COLOUR 3
 70 COLOUR 2+128
 80 GCOL 1,4
 90 GCOL 4,128+5
100 MOVE 123,345
110 MOVE 234,421
120 VDU 29,500;490;
130 FOR M%=0 TO 255
140 A%(M%,T%)=?(&300+M%)
150 NEXT M%
160 NEXT T%
170 @%=4
180 VDU 2
190 MODE 0
200 FOR M%=0 TO 255
210 PRINT "|";~M%+&300;" |";
220 FOR T%=0 TO 7
```

```
230 PRINT A%(M%,T%);
240 NEXT T%
250 PRINT "  |"'"|";TAB(39);"|"'STRING$
(40,"-")
260 NEXT M%
270 VDU 3
```

As you can see, the section from lines 40 to 120 set up various
parameters, to give something distinctive to look for in each mode. For
example, if we later find a byte holding 17, we could be right in
assuming that it has something to do with the text window in line 40
(the complete printout from this program appears at the end of the
chapter). The problem is that none of those statements make the
screen scroll, so the value in &320 could be the top of page address.
Both are the same before scrolling takes place. So, to see which it is,
scroll the screen a few times, and then investigate the contents of
these locations again. You will see that they haven't changed so this
location must store the lowest address used by the current screen
mode.

Having discovered that, the next step is to see what happens when we
alter this location. Try putting the machine in mode 4, and then typing
'?&321 = &F'. This is telling the computer that video RAM starts at
location &F00. But nothing happens after you do this. Try typing
'CLS'. After you do this the screen will do anything but clear. You'll
probably see a lot of garbage on it. Ignore all the rubbish for a
moment, and type 'CLG'. The rubbish will disappear. The trouble is,
the CLS mechanism is carried out by the ULA, and it has not been told
that VDU RAM has moved so at every CLS, it will clear the wrong area
of memory. The 6845 will now have moved VDU RAM to start at
location &F00. The other problem is that the ULA will scroll the screen
wrongly, so returning you to the 'real' mode 4 screen after you scroll
into the start of it. The upshot of this is that you can select other pages
of memory for display, but don't then scroll the screen. It is alright if
you define a text window to occupy the whole new page, since
scrolling in a window does not move the VDU RAM around, but it is
rather slow.

The application for having more than one page of screen memory that
first occured to me was to construct an animation program, which
could switch rapidly between two images on different pages, to give
the illusion of movement.

You will find that getting mode 7 to display in other pages is often very
confusing, and does not work out exactly as planned. I would advise
you to steer clear of this activity. The other danger spot occurs when
you overwrite your program and a new screen page. Typing CLG will
destroy your program.

Locations &322 and &323 — Address of top left of screen. (16 bits). LSB MSB

The contents of these two locations in each of the screen modes are as follows:

Mode —	0	1	2	3	4	5	6	7
Contents —	12288	12288	12288	16384	22528	22528	24576	31744

The contents are the same as in locations &320 and &321. However, as we've already found the start of VDU RAM location, it would be safe to assume that this location contains the address of the top left of the screen. If you scroll the screen a little, and then print the value in these locations, you will find that it has changed, reinforcing this view.

Machine language programmers will find the contents of this location useful, since without it, they would have severe problems in POKEing data directly to the screen. For BASIC programmers, any use of this location has been removed by the existing system software.

Altering this location does nothing useful, but is a fairly harmless occupation.

Locations &324 to &325 — Bytes per line. (16 bits). LSB MSB

The contents of these two locations in each of the eight screen modes are as follows:

Mode —	0	1	2	3	4	5	6	7
Contents —	640	640	640	640	320	320	320	40

From the values given for modes 0 and 4, you would expect these locations to hold the horizontal graphics resolution in the current screen mode. From the value given for mode 7, you would be forgiven for thinking that these locations hold the number of characters per line. But if you remember from the last chapter when I said that modes 0 to 3 have 80 characters per line, and modes 4,5 and 6 have 40 characters per line, you should see some pattern in the above values. Also, 20K divided by 32 lines gives 640, and 10K divided by 32 lines gives 320. You may now be able to see why this location contains the number of bytes per line of text. These locations are used, in conjunction with some others, to decide what the graphics resolution of the current screen mode is.

Altering the contents of these locations alters the number of bytes scrolled. Thus, if you execute '?&324 = 20', while in mode 7, and then try to scroll, you will get some very odd effects. Similarly, in any of the graphics modes, altering the value in these locations gives the computer a funny idea of the resolution of the current mode, and so all plotting looks a little odd. The application of this is that you can alter the number of characters per line, by a method similar to that outlined at the end of the last chapter. These locations go some of the way towards telling the MOS that you have made the alteration. As an example, try this program:

```
10 REM Order out of chaos
20 REM Copyright (C) 1982
30 REM Jeremy Ruston
40 MODE 4
50 REM Kid the system about the
60 REM graphics resolution...
70 ?&324=32
80 REM There are now 288 bytes/line
90 REM Or 288/8=36 chars/line
```

```
100 FOR T=0 TO 100
110 DRAW RND(1280)-1,RND(1024)-1
120 NEXT T
130 COLOUR 0
140 COLOUR 129
150 PRINT ''"Press the space bar"
160 REPEAT
170 REPEAT UNTIL GET=32
180 REM Give the screen 36 chars/line
190 VDU 23,0,1,36,0,0,0,0,0,0,0
200 REPEAT UNTIL GET=32
210 REM And take it back.
220 VDU 23,0,1,40,0,0,0,0,0,0,0
230 UNTIL FALSE
```

Locations &326 and &327 — Screen memory length. (16 bits.) LSB MSB

The contents are as follows:

Mode —	0	1	2	3	4	5	6	7
Contents —	20480	20480	20480	16384	10240	10240	8192	1024

This one is a bit of a cinch. The 1024 for mode 7 and the 20480 for mode 0 give this away as the length of screen memory.

The value stored here is used when the 6845 is used for scrolling. It contains the number of bytes that can be scrolled before registers 12 and 13 will have to be reset to their starting values.

Location &328 — Top right y-coordinate of text window. (8 bits).

This location will always contain zero, unless a text window has been defined, in which case it will contain the last parameter of the VDU 28 statement.

Altering the contents of this location will serve no useful purpose, except save you the trouble of a VDU 28 statement. This is not advisable — remember the golden rule: only use the indirection operators (?) when you have no other choice.

Location &329 — Top right x-coordinate of text window. (8 bits).

This location normally contains one less than the number of characters per line in each mode:

Mode	0	1	2	3	4	5	6	7
Contents	79	39	19	79	39	19	39	39

If a text window has been defined, it contains the third parameter of the VDU 28 statement.

Location &32A — Bottom left y-coordinate of text window. (8 bits).

This location normally contains the number of lines minus one in the current screen.

Mode —	0	1	2	3	4	5	6	7
Contents —	31	31	31	24	31	31	24	24

If a text window has been defined, this location contains the second parameter of the VDU 28 statement.

Location &32B — Bottom left x-coordinate of text window. (8 bits).

This location normally contains zero, but after a text window has been defined, it contains the first parameter of the VDU 28 statement.

Location &32C — Cursor X-coordinate. (8 bits).

This location contains the X−coordinate of the text cursor, from the top left of the screen. Thus, after a CLS or a cursor home, it is initialized to the contents of location &32B. Reading the variable POS gives the value stored here, minus the value stored in location &32B.

Altering this value gives you one way of altering the cursor's position, but there are more elegant ways.

Location &32D — Cursor Y-coordinate (8 bits)

This location holds the Y-coordinate of the cursor, with reference to the top left of the screen. Thus after a CLS or cursor home it is initialized to the contents of location &328. Reading VPOS gives the value stored here, minus the value in &328.

Locations &32E and &32F — Cursor address. (16 bits). LSB MSB

Initially, the contents of this location are:

Mode	—	0	1	2	3	4	5	6	7
Contents	—		12288	12288	12288	16384	22528	22528	24576	31744

But, with the program given earlier to list out the contents of memory locations after various windows had been defined, different results were obtained:

Mode	—	0	1	2	3	4	5	6	7
Contents	—		14216	14224	14240	18312	23496	23504	25544	31865

So, I was faced with a number which was the top left-hand address of VDU RAM before any text windows were in force, and altered in the presence of a window. I concluded that this was the address of the cursor. Some experimentation proved me right for example, if you execute the statements '?(?&32E + (?&32F)*256) = 33' in mode 7, you will be rewarded by seeing an exclamation mark appear on the screen under the line you typed, to be rapidly replaced with the prompt. You can stop the prompt obscuring things by appending the statement 'VDU 30' to the end of the instructions. This will return the cursor to the top left-hand corner of the screen, after the initial statement has been executed.

Locations &330 and &331 — Top right y-coordinate of graphics window. (16 bits). MSB LSB

The contents of this location in all eight modes are as follows:

Mode —	0	1	2	3	4	5	6	7
Contents —	108	108	108	108	108	108	108	108

These two locations first interested me when I was looking for the place where the last argument of the VDU 24 statement was stored. In the program I used to get these figures, given earlier in the chapter, you will recall that the last parameter was the number 432. Thus, I was looking for two locations which collectively contained 432. I was not in luck, so I turned my mind to seeing how else the required information could be stored.

All graphics statements operate on a grid of 1280 by 1024. So the vertical scaling factor was four, since 256 (the vertical resolution in all modes) into 1024 goes four times. So maybe I should look for a location containing 432/4 (108) instead. This I did, and before long came up with these locations. To test this, I checked that these locations contained 255 before a graphics window was created.

The primary use of a location such as this is to be able to see what the size of the current graphics window is, without having to save the required information in variables. I would not recommend altering this location by any other means than the VDU 24 statement, simply to aid readability in your programs. If you ever read this location in a program, I would suggest you use a function like this, for the same reasons:

```
10 REM A function to read the vertical
20 REM dimensions of the current
30 REM graphics window.
40 REM Copyright (C) Jeremy Ruston
50 MODE 4
60 PRINT 'FNvert
70 PRINT ''"The answer is given as "
```

```
  80 PRINT '"1020 since it has been "
  90 PRINT '"scaled by four."
 100 END
1000 DEF FNvert=(?&331)*4
```

Locations &332 and &333 — Top right X-coordinate of graphics window. (16 bits). MSB LSB

Using the same program as before, the results obtained were:

Mode	—	Ø	1	2	3	4	5	6	7
Contents	—	266	133	66	66	133	66	33	66

Remember the order in which the bytes describing the text window are presented, I was expecting to find the top right X-coordinate of the graphics window at these locations. The VDU 24 statement in the program gave this as 532. The horizontal scaling factors for each of the eight modes are as follows:

Mode	—	Ø	1	2	3	4	5	6	7
Scaling factor	—	2	4	8	X	4	8	X	X

(X = don't care)

So, 532/2 = 266, 532/4 = 133 and 532/8 = 66 (whole number part only). So this location does indeed hold that information, but only in terms of the actual graphics grid of 640 by 256, 320 by 256 or whatever, and not the normal grid of 1280 by 1024.

The same points I made after the last location hold true for this one, with regard to interrogation and alteration.

Locations &334 and &335 — Bottom right Y-coordinate of graphics window. (16 bits). MSB LSB

This one was very predictable. The values I found were all 12 (12*4 = 48, is the nearest number to 50 divisible by four, and 50 is the second parameter in the VDU 24 statement). So this location contains the bottom right Y-coordinate of the current graphics coordinate, in terms of a vertical resolution of 256, rather than 1024. The same points about altering and interrogation as made in the discussion of location &330 hold true.

Locations &336 and &337 — Bottom right X-coordinate of graphics window. (16 bits). MSB LSB

With the same provisos as mentioned for location &332, this location holds the first parameter of the VDU 24 statement, the bottom right X-coordinate of the current graphics window.

Don't forget about the scaling factors in all the modes.

Locations &338 and &339 — Y-coordinate of graphics origin. (16 bits). MSB LSB

In all modes, the program gave the contents of these locations as 490, which I gave as the Y-coordinate of the graphics origin in the VDU 29 statement. Normally this location contains zero, because the origin is at the bottom left-hand corner of the screen.

Altering this location is again pretty pointless, but interrogating it can often be useful. Do remember to use a special function, rather than using the indirection operators directly, if only for reasons of elegance.

Locations &33A and &33B — X-coordinate of graphics origin. (16 bits). MSB LSB

These locations contain 500 in all modes, which I gave as the first parameter of the VDU 29 statement in the program. So it contains the X-coordinate of the graphics origin, but without scaling, ie it contains the X-coordinate directly in all modes, not divided by two in mode Ø, and 4 in modes 1 and 4.

Locations &33C and &33D — Current Y-coordinate of graphics cursor. (16 bits). MSB LSB

These locations contain 421 in all graphics modes, and 50 in the text only modes. The 421 is instantly recognizable as the second coordinate given in the MOVE statement in the program.

I had only found the most recently visited point, I still had to find the point visited before last, which is used by the PLOT 85 routines.

Altering this quantity is easily done by using the MOVE statement, or any other of the PLOT statements. It is often useful to read the current coordinates though, so I suggest you use a function to do this.

Locations &33E and &33F — Current X-coordinate of graphics cursor. (16 bits).
MSB LSB

In graphics modes, this location contains 234 according to the program given earlier, and 60 in the non-graphics modes. 234 is, of course, the first parameter of the second MOVE statement in the program. As with the previous location, it is initialized to zero at a mode change or CLG.

The points about interrogation and alteration made in the discussion of the previous location hold true for this one as well.

Location &367 — Current screen mode. (8 bits).

The contents of this location are:

Mode	—	0	1	2	3	4	5	6	7
Contents	—	0	1	2	3	4	5	6	7

I need hardly say more.

The location does not seem to affect anything if you alter it, but reading it can be useful, since it is then possible to write a graphics program which the user can start running in whatever mode he or she likes, and the program can see what mode is being used, and scale its output accordingly.

Location &36B — Flags one. (8 bits).

This location was a pest to work out. It normally contains zero, but when running the program, I found it contained 8. I started looking for something in the program which involved the figure 8, to see what this location was doing. I found nothing, so I resorted to the old and tested method of randomly placing values in the location. I started out by putting the machine in mode 4, and then executing '?&36B = 1'. No sooner had I done that then the printer I was using, and had de-selected with CTRL-C, popped into life. It then became obvious that the location contained eight flags, so I began working out what the other flags were for.

The next step was to put two in the location, to test the second bit, and see what happens. This I did, and found out only that the screen refused to scroll, as if it was in VDU 5 mode. It wasn't in VDU 5 mode, because the cursor was still present, and the text colour was still selectable by means of the COLOUR statement. So bit 1 determined whether scrolling was to take place.

Bit 2 was a little easier to discover. I put the computer in page mode, and looked at the contents of the location. I was rewarded by seeing it contained the figure 4.

Bit 3 was difficult, so I just placed the number 8 in &36B, and saw what happened. The screen started scrolling by moving the contents of memory locations. So this was the 'kind of scroll flag' I mentioned at the beginning of the chapter. Try it and see.

Bit 4 does not do anything in the present operating system.

Bit 5 is the joined/separate text/graphics cursors flag. When set to true, VDU 5 mode is active.

Bit 6 appears to be the edit mode on/off flag.

Bit 7 is the VDU driver's disable/enable flag. When set, the VDU drivers are inactive, and will remain so until a VDU 6 instruction is executed, or until the flag is set to zero.

Except for bits 1 and 3, it is easier to set these flags by executing the appropriate VDU commands. However, reading them is feasible and often useful.

Setting bit 1 is useful if you want to print on the bottom line of the screen, since normally the screen has a tendency to scroll if you do this, especially with the bottom right-hand character position.

Setting bit 3 to a full scroll when you have a text window in operation is interesting. Try setting up a text window of just the top left character position, by executing 'VDU 28,0,0,0,0', and then type '?&36B = 0'. Then, every time you press a key, the whole screen will roll up, unless you hit CTRL-H, delete or CTRL-K, in which case it will roll down. This is an easier way of rolling than using the 6845's registers and 12 and 13 directly, but does have the disadvantage of leaving a trail of characters up the left most column of the screen. If you just use 'PRINT' to roll the screen, under program control, the problem is removed, except that now, all the text in the left most column of the screen will be cleared.

Location &36D — CLS/scroll filler byte. (8 bits).

The contents of this location in the eight modes are as follows:

Mode	— 0	1	2	3	4	5	6	7
Contents	— 0	0	0	0	0	0	0	32

Go into mode 7, and try typing '?&36D = 42', then clear the screen.

This location holds the byte that will be put into every memory location as it is scrolled or cleared. Thus in mode 7, the code for a space, 32, is used, but in other modes, 0 is used since 0 corresponds to a byte completely made up of colour 0, presuming colour 0 is the current background colour.

In one of the modes 0 to 6, try '?&36D = &AA', and then clearing the screen. You should get some sort of stripy background, since the binary of &AA is 10101010. If you alter the background character, the edit keys do not work correctly, or rather the copy key does not. The technique is still useful, for shading if nothing else. In mode 7, you could try typing in response to a progam like this:

```
10 REM Copyright (C) Jeremy Ruston
20 REPEAT
30 ?&36D=GET
40 CLS
50 UNTIL FALSE
60 REM Line 30 could also be :
70 PRINT TAB(0,24)
```

Location &36E — Graphics foreground colour mask. (8 bits).

The program I used to list the content of various memory locations contained the line GCOL 1,4, so when I started to look for the location that held the current graphics colour, I first looked for a location that contained 4 in all modes. But there aren't four colours in all modes. Colour 4 in modes 0 and 4 is in fact the same as colour 0, and in modes 1 and 5 it is the same as colour zero, for a slightly different reason. I therefore started looking for a location containing something like this in all the graphics modes:

Mode	—	0	1	2	4	5
Contents	—	0	0	4	0	0

However, if you look, there is no such location. The alternatives for storing the colour directly are few — namely a 'colour mask' can be used, as is employed in the Acorn Atom.

A colour mask is a byte equivalent to a byte of the display memory containing just the current colour. Refer back to the description of byte mapping in the previous chapter, and working from those tables, make up a byte of the colour the new graphics foreground colour is to be. You will then have a colour mask for that colour.

For example, in the two colour modes, a mask for colour 0 is a byte containing zero, and the mask for colour one is a byte containing 255. The best way to see this is to examine masks that the computer makes up for you. You do this by changing the graphics foreground colour to the desired colour, and then the contents of &36E is the mask for that colour.

A little bit of experimentation (ie making up colour masks by hand and then looking for them) showed that the graphics foreground mask is stored at address &36E.

The computer uses the mask in combination with some boolean operations to speed up the plotting operation, the exact process of which is irrelevant.

Reading the current foreground colour from this location is a tiresome business, but here are some routines to do it:

```
10 REM GCOL 0,X read functions.
20 REM Use the one appropriate to
30 REM your current mode.
1000 DEF FNtwo_colour_modes=?&36E AND 1
2000 DEF FNfour_colour_modes=(?&36E AND
1)+(?&36E AND 16)/8
3000 DEF FNmode_two LOCAL T,B
3010 FOR T=0 TO 6 STEP 2
3020 IF (2^T AND ?&36E)=2^T THEN B=B+2^
(T/2)
3030 NEXT T
3040=B
```

Altering this location is great fun. For example, this program gives you striped text, by setting the graphics foreground mask, and then printing under the influence of VDU 5.

```
10 MODE 5
20 ?&36E=&5A
30 VDU 5
40 PRINT'''"There's a lady who's sure
all that glit-ters is gold"'
50 PRINT "And she's buying a   stairwa
y to heaven.."
60 VDU 4
70 END
```

Location &36F — Graphics background colour mask. (8 bits).

This location is the exact opposite of location &36E, in that it determines the current graphics background colour, rather than the current foreground colour. The format of the location is exactly the same, and it can be read from using the same routines as location &36E, except you'll have to change every occurence of &36E to &36F.

The application of this location is to enable you to fill whole areas of the screen with a striped pattern, in the same way as you fill in rectangles at the moment, using VDU 24, followed by GCOL. Just set the background colour mask beforehand to a striped pattern, and you'll have a striped rectangle.

Location &370 —
Graphics foreground
modifier. (8 bits).

This location contains the first parameter of the most recent GCOL
statement setting the graphics foreground colour. There's not much
you can usefully do with it, except possible read it. If you set it to an
out-of-range value, ie 5 or above, you get some pretty weird results
with your next plot, but there again, why not just make the first
parameter of the GCOL statement out of range?

Location &371 — Graphics background modifier. (8 bits).

When George Mikes wrote his definitive 'How to be an Alien', which describes in great detail the shortcomings of the British, through the eyes of a foreigner, the chapter entitled 'Sex' contained just the following words: "On the continent they have sex; the British have hot water bottles." The chapter has come in for a little criticism since then.

The point of all this is that I can find as little to write about with reference to this location as George Mikes could about the Great British sex life.

Location &375 — Colours available. (8 bits).

This location contains one less than the number of colours available in the current mode, except for mode 7, where it contains zero. Thus its contents in the eight modes are as follows:

Mode —	0	1	2	3	4	5	6	7
Contents —	1	3	15	1	1	3	1	0

The effect of altering this register is dramatic. If you increase it to the maximum of 15 in any mode other than 2 and 7, you'll get rather big writing. This technique is not perfect, since the letters overlap. I'll show you a better program in a few pages.

An odd thing is that after altering this register, to get VDU 19 working correctly, you'll find you have to alter the colour of two of the logical colours to get any proper change in colour of a single actual colour.

Location &376 — Bytes per character. (8 bits).

This location holds the number of bytes that separate the top of one character from the bottom of the next. Its contents in the eight modes are as follows:

Mode —	0	1	2	3	4	5	6	7
Contents —	8	16	32	8	8	16	8	1

In mode 7, typing '?&376 = 2' will space out the text you type across the line by a factor of two. The trouble is, when the computer reaches the end of a screen line, it doesn't quite know where to go next, since it is sure there are 40 characters to every line, but it's only managed to fit 20 on. So the remedy is to tell it that there are now only 20 characters on each screen line. Rather then setting up a text window, try using '?&329 = 19' to set the right-hand margin to 19. This will ensure that normal 6845 scrolling is carried out, even though there is a screen window. In other modes, you can get pretty overlapping text by reducing the number normally held in this location. Not altogether useful.

Here is the 'funny writing' program, properly debugged:

```
 10 REM Funny writing
 20 REM Copyright (C) 1982
 30 REM Jeremy Ruston
 40 MODE 0
 50 ?&375=15
 60 ?&376=32
 70 ?&377=1
 80 ?&329=19
 90 PRINT TAB(0,13);
100 PROCCENTRE("T H E")
110 PRINT
120 PROCCENTRE("B B C")
130 PRINT
140 PROCCENTRE("M I C R O")
150 PRINT
160 PROCCENTRE("R E V E A L E D")
170 PRINT
180 END
190 DEF PROCCENTRE(A$)
```

```
200 PRINT TAB(10-LEN(A$)/2);A$
210 ENDPROC
```

Location &377 — Pixels per byte. (8 bits).

This location contains zero in the non graphics modes, and the number of pixels per byte minus one in the other modes. Thus its contents in the eight modes are as follows:

Mode —	0	1	2	3	4	5	6	7
Contents —	7	3	1	0	7	3	0	0

The data stored here is used only in graphics commands. Altering it just causes some bizarre effects without doing anything useful.

It is possible to use this location in conjunction with a couple of those we've already discussed to work out the graphics resolution of the current mode, bearing in mind that the vertical resolution is constant at 256 for all modes.

Location &37E —
Perma-edit. (8 bits).

This location normally contains 13, but I found that if you load 127 into it, you can stop the computer dropping you out of edit mode at every carriage return. I use this feature when I am copying a number of lines from the top of the screen to the bottom, since it allows me to dispense with moving the cursor back up the screen to start copying each new line.

Location &382 — Define flags. (8 bits).

These flags control whether a RAM-based, or ROM-based character generator shall be used for a particular set of characters. If any of the bits indicated below are set to '1', the corresponding region of the character set will be read from RAM, else from ROM.

The bits control the following section of the set:

Bit	ROM location	RAM location	Character range
0	—	&C00 to &CFF	224–255
1	—	&1000 to &10FF	192–223
2	—	&1100 to &11FF	160–191
3	—	&1200 to &12FF	128–159
4	&C200 to &C2FF	&1300 to &13FF	96–127
5	&C100 to &C1FF	&1400 to &14FF	64– 95
6	&C000 to &C0FF	&1500 to &15FF	32– 63

If the later portion of the character set, ie that from 128 to 255, is set to a ROM–based character generator, it takes the normal ASCII set as its starting point, but displaced by 128.

The advantage of this location is that by setting it to zero you can undo all the re-defining you have done, which is just not possible with the present ROM revision normally.

On the subject of the character generator, here is a routine to print out the entire character set, eight times the normal size.

```
10 MODE 7
20 FOR T%=&C000 TO &C2FF
30 IF (T%-&C000) MOD 8=0 THEN
   PRINT "-----------"
40 FOR A%=7 TO 0 STEP -1
50 IF (2^A% AND ?T%)=2^A%
   THEN VDU 255 ELSE VDU 32
60 NEXT A%
70 PRINT
80 NEXT T%
```

Location &D8 — Caps lock/shift lock. (8 bits).

This location contains 32 when caps lock is active, 16 when shift lock is active and 48 when neither are active. It is also possible to set the location from BASIC to simulate the pressing of the required key, but for some weird reason a character 13 has to be printed before the relevant lights are lit.

The application of this would be to ensure that the user of a program only typed in upper or lower case by setting the contents of &D8 before the INPUT statement is executed.

Under some more peculiar conditions, this location can be used to sense whether control or shift are active, but I would recommend using INKEY with a negative argument to achieve the same result.

Locations &38A to &399 — Current palette. (16 bytes).

These 16 locations hold the actual colour of each of the 16 logical colours. Thus the actual colour of colour zero is stored in address &38A, the actual colour of colour 1 in address &38B and so on up to the actual colour of logical colour 15 being stored in location &399. Obviously only mode 2 uses all the locations. The sample run shows the default settings of this table, but remember that only the first two or four numbers are significant in the majority of modes. The contents of the table can be altered with VDU 19, which also changes the colours on the screen.

Altering this table has no effect at all. Reading from it can be useful in a lot of cases. For example, this routine calls up mode 4, and then chooses random background and foreground colours, but uses this table to ensure that the colours are never the same.

```
10 MODE 4
20 VDU 19,0,RND(8)-1,0,0,0
30 REPEAT
40 VDU 19,1,RND(8)-1,0,0,0
50 UNTIL ?&38B<>?&38A
```

You can get a similar effect by using one of the MOS calls detailed in the User Guide.

The remaining two areas
of interest are buffers:

Buffers are used to store data between being processed by some peripheral and being read by the computer, or the other way around. For example, most printers print characters at around 100 characters per second. The computer can print characters at a far greater speed, however. To stop the computer being constantly tied up with sending characters to the printer, it stores characters in a temporary storage area, the buffer, if the printer is not ready to accept the characters. They can be sent to the printer when the computer receives word that it is ready. If the buffer does ever get filled up, the computer's operation is suspended, until it can empty the buffer.

The keyboard buffer is used to store characters issued when the computer is to busy to process them, so it, in effect, operates as the exact complement of the Centronics buffer.

The Centronics (R) buffer starts at address &3A0 and extends to address &3DF.

The run time keyboard buffer starts at address &3E0 and finishes at address &3FF. The contents of address &23C hold the next free location in the buffer, minus &300. When the pointer gets past 255, it reverts to 224, the decimal equivalent of &E0. Thus to insert a character into the buffer, you need only put the character in the address given by &300 plus the contents of &23C then increment the contents of &23C, remembering to reset it to 224, if it passes 255.

This program shows how to do it:

```
  10 DIM START 200
  20 REM This program dumped itself on
  30 REM the printer.
  40 PROCKEY(0,"WIDTH 40 |M |B LIST |M
|C WIDTH 0 |M")
  50 PROCADD(CHR$(144))
  60 END
1000 DEF PROCADD(A$)
1010 LOCAL B$,T,A
1020 IF LEN(A$)>32 THEN ENDPROC
1030 FOR T=1 TO LEN(A$)
1040 B$=MID$(A$,T,1)
```

```
1050 A=?&23C
1060 ?(&300+A)=ASC(B$)
1070 A=A+1
1080 IF A>255 THEN A=224
1090 ?&23C=A
1100 NEXT T
1110 ENDPROC
2000 DEF PROCKEY(N,A$)
2010 $START="*KEY "+STR$(N)+CHR$(34)+A$
+CHR$(34)
2020 X%=START MOD 256
2030 Y%=START DIV 256
2040 CALL &FFF7
2050 ENDPROC
```

PROCADD will add the characters in A$ to the buffer. When a program returns to an INPUT statement, or ends the characters in the buffer will be used as input, as if they had been typed in at the keyboard. The example program uses this feature to list itself out on the printer.

The disadvantage of PROCADD is that it only works with 32 characters, which is a little restrictive, so I have defined a procedure to define a key with a BASIC string, to make up for *KEY 0 A$ being illegal. Then the code for function key 0 can be put into the buffer, and it only takes up a single character. The function keys have codes from 144 to 154. The cursor control keys and the copy keys are stored in the buffer using the same codes as they generate under *FX4,1.

Try replacing the text in line 40 with anything else, and see what happens. Don't forget that you'll lose any previous text stored under key zero.

At the beginning of the chapter, I listed the current text colour as something to find in the region &300 to &3FF. After research, you'll find that the current text colour is not stored in this area — this can be verified by using this program.

```
10 MODE 5
20 COLOUR 2
30 COLOUR 128+1
40 PRINT "COLOUR 2"
50 DIM M% 255
60 FOR T%=0 TO 255
70 M%?T%=T%?&300
```

```
 80 NEXT T%
 90 MODE 5
100 PRINT "COLOUR 2 ?"
110 FOR T%=0 TO 255
120 T%?&300=T%?M%
130 NEXT T%
```

The program takes you into mode 5, sets the text background and foreground colours and then takes you back into mode 5. After the text colour is set, the contents of memory from &300 to &3FF is stored, and then these values are written back after the mode is changed back to five. You will find that even though the contents of &300 to &3FF are identical in both cases, the text colour is different.

Having established that I had to look elsewhere I used the routine given in section one to make mode 0 VDU RAM start at address zero. Then I made various changes to the text background and foreground colours, and looked around for the locations affected. Having a video monitor, I could locate the locations easily. They were &CD and &CE. As they are zero page locations, they are quick to access in machine code, so it shows how much Acorn wanted to optimize the speed of text printing. It might have been a good idea to have stored the graphics background and foreground colours in page zero as well, since it is just as important to speed up the graphics routines as the text.

The next stage was to work out how these locations held the colours.

I used this program to list out the contents of these locations under various colour combinations, in a four colour mode, mode 5:

```
 10 MODE 5
 20 FOR FRONT=0 TO 3
 30 FOR BACK=0 TO 3
 40 COLOUR FRONT
 50 COLOUR BACK+128
 60 PRINT "FRONT=";FRONT,"BACK=";BACK;
 70 PRINT ?&CD,?&CE
 80 NEXT BACK
 90 NEXT FRONT
100 END
RUN
FRONT=0    BACK=0         255              255
FRONT=0    BACK=1         240              255
```

FRONT=0	BACK=2	15	255
FRONT=0	BACK=3	0	255
FRONT=1	BACK=0	240	240
FRONT=1	BACK=1	255	240
FRONT=1	BACK=2	0	240
FRONT=1	BACK=3	15	240
FRONT=2	BACK=0	15	15
FRONT=2	BACK=1	0	15
FRONT=2	BACK=2	255	15
FRONT=2	BACK=3	240	15
FRONT=3	BACK=0	0	0
FRONT=3	BACK=1	15	0
FRONT=3	BACK=2	240	0
FRONT=3	BACK=3	255	0

The program will only work if you've got a printer, because it involves printing in colour 1 on a colour 129 background, which is, of course, unreadable.

You might have been expecting the two locations to be colour masks for the background and foreground colours. The above table will tell you that that is not the case. In addition, altering location &CE alters both the foreground and background colours, as you can easily verify.

There does not appear to be any recognizable pattern in the values, so I resorted to an old trick of displaying everything in binary. The program and printout appear as:

```
 10 MODE 5
 20 FOR BACK=0 TO 3
 30 FOR FRONT=0 TO 3
 40 COLOUR FRONT
 50 COLOUR BACK+128
 60 PRINT "BACK=";FNB2(BACK),"FRONT=";
FNB2(FRONT);
 70 PRINT ,FNBIN(?&CD),FNBIN(?&CE)
 80 NEXT FRONT
 90 NEXT BACK
100 END
110 DEF FNB2(A)
120 LOCAL T,B$
130 FOR T=1 TO 0 STEP -1
```

```
   140 IF (2^T AND A)=2^T THEN B$=B$+"1"
ELSE B$=B$+"0"
   150 NEXT T
   160=B$
   170 DEF FNBIN(A)
   180 LOCAL B$,T
   190 FOR T=7 TO 0 STEP -1
   200 IF (2^T AND A)=2^T THEN B$=B$+"1"
ELSE B$=B$+"0"
   210 NEXT T
   220=B$
>RUN
BACK=00     FRONT=00    11111111    11111111
BACK=00     FRONT=01    11110000    11110000
BACK=00     FRONT=10    00001111    00001111
BACK=00     FRONT=11    00000000    00000000
BACK=01     FRONT=00    11110000    11111111
BACK=01     FRONT=01    11111111    11110000
BACK=01     FRONT=10    00000000    00001111
BACK=01     FRONT=11    00001111    00000000
BACK=10     FRONT=00    00001111    11111111
BACK=10     FRONT=01    00000000    11110000
BACK=10     FRONT=10    11111111    00001111
BACK=10     FRONT=11    11110000    00000000
BACK=11     FRONT=00    00000000    11111111
BACK=11     FRONT=01    00001111    11110000
BACK=11     FRONT=10    11110000    00001111
BACK=11     FRONT=11    11111111    00000000
```

Again, this program does not run too well if you don't have a printer. You could, however, store all results in an array, and then display them in mode 7 to make up for this deficiency.

The third column of the printout is the contents of &CD, and the next is the contents of &CE. At this point, it would be helpful to reproduce the colour masks of colours 0 to 3 (these are for the four colour modes):

```
COLOUR 0   00000000
COLOUR 1   00001111
COLOUR 2   11110000
COLOUR 3   11111111
```

81

You will notice that the contents of location &CE is the inverse of the foreground colour mask. After a little thought, you may notice that the contents of location &CD is NOT (foreground mask EOR background mask). This may sound a complicated arrangement, but it only means that where a bit of the foreground mask is '1' and the same bit of the background mask is '0', the same bit in &CD is a '0'. If, however, the two bits of the masks are the same (ie both '1's or both '0's), the same bit in &CD will be a '1'.

Thus, the computer is free to use the foreground mask almost as it stands, but to get the background mask, it has to use the contents of &CD (EOR) and the contents of &CE'.

The same is true for the two and 16 colour modes, except of course the number of pixels controlled by each byte is different.

If you use this location to get striped text, without recourse to VDU 5 mode, remember that you'll also have to alter location &36D, to be the background colour mask, to ensure that when you scroll the screen, or clear it, it clears to whatever pattern you chose.

Whilst trying to design envelopes, you may find that your best one has been lost, by being scrolled off the screen as you type the SOUND statements to test it. This program allows you to recall from memory any of the four envelopes.

```
 10 REM Envelope recall
 20 REM (C) Jeremy Ruston 1982
 30 REM --------------------
 40 INPUT "Enter the number of the ENV
ELOPE "NUM
 50 @%=0
 60 PRINT "The envelope is:"
 70 PRINT "ENVELOPE ";NUM;
 80 FOR T=0 TO 12
 90 PRINT ",";?(&800+NUM*16+T);
100 NEXT T
110 PRINT
120 @%=10
```

```
|300 |  255  255  255  255  255  255  255  255 |
|                                              |
 ----------------------------------------------
|301 |  255  255  255  255  255  255  255  255 |
|                                              |
 ----------------------------------------------
|302 |  255  255  255  255  255  255  255  255 |
|                                              |
 ----------------------------------------------
|303 |  255  255  255  255  255  255  255  255 |
|                                              |
 ----------------------------------------------
|304 |  255  255  255  255  255  255  255  255 |
|                                              |
 ----------------------------------------------
|305 |  255  255  255  255  255  255  255  255 |
|                                              |
 ----------------------------------------------
|306 |  255  255  255  255  255  255  255  255 |
|                                              |
 ----------------------------------------------
|307 |   25   25   25   25   25   25   25   25 |
|                                              |
 ----------------------------------------------
|308 |    0    0    0    0    0    0    0    0 |
|                                              |
 ----------------------------------------------
|309 |  255  255  255  255  255  255  255  255 |
|                                              |
 ----------------------------------------------
|30A |  255  255  255  255  255  255  255  255 |
|                                              |
 ----------------------------------------------
|30B |  255  255  255  255  255  255  255  255 |
|                                              |
 ----------------------------------------------
|30C |  255  255  255  255  255  255  255  255 |
|                                              |
 ----------------------------------------------
|30D |  255  255  255  255  255  255  255  255 |
|                                              |
 ----------------------------------------------
```

```
|30E |  255  255  255  255  255  255  255  255  |
|    |                                          |
-----------------------------------------------
|30F |  255  255  255  255  255  255  255  255  |
|    |                                          |
-----------------------------------------------
|310 |  255  255  255  255  255  255  255  255  |
|    |                                          |
-----------------------------------------------
|311 |  255  255  255  255  255  255  255  255  |
|    |                                          |
-----------------------------------------------
|312 |  255  255  255  255  255  255  255  255  |
|    |                                          |
-----------------------------------------------
|313 |  255  255  255  255  255  255  255  255  |
|    |                                          |
-----------------------------------------------
|314 |  255  255  255  255  255  255  255  255  |
|    |                                          |
-----------------------------------------------
|315 |  255  255  255  255  255  255  255  255  |
|    |                                          |
-----------------------------------------------
|316 |  255  255  255  255  255  255  255  255  |
|    |                                          |
-----------------------------------------------
|317 |  255  255  255  255  255  255  255  255  |
|    |                                          |
-----------------------------------------------
|318 |  255  255  255  255  255  255  255  255  |
|    |                                          |
-----------------------------------------------
|319 |  255  255  255  255  255  255  255  255  |
|    |                                          |
-----------------------------------------------
|31A |  255  255  255  255  255  255  255  255  |
|    |                                          |
-----------------------------------------------
|31B |  255  255  255  255  255  255  255  255  |
|    |                                          |
-----------------------------------------------
```

31C	255	255	255	255	255	255	255	255

31D	255	255	255	255	255	255	255	255

31E	255	255	255	255	255	255	255	255

31F	255	255	255	255	255	255	255	255

320	0	0	0	0	0	0	0	0
LSB Screen memory start								

321	48	48	48	64	88	88	96	124
MSB Screen memory start								

322	0	0	0	0	0	0	0	0
LSB Address of top left of screen								

323	48	48	48	64	88	88	96	124
MSB Address of top left of screen								

324	128	128	128	128	64	64	64	40
LSB Bytes per line (whole screen)								

325	2	2	2	2	1	1	1	0
MSB Bytes per line (whole screen)								

326	0	0	0	0	0	0	0	0
LSB Screen memory length								

327	80	80	80	64	40	40	32	4
MSB Screen memory length								

328	3	3	3	3	3	3	3	3
Y-coord of top right of text window								

329	17	17	17	17	17	17	17	17
X-coord of top right of text window								

32A	20	20	20	20	20	20	20	20
Y-coord of bottom left of text window								

32B	1	1	1	1	1	1	1	1
X-coord of bottom left of text screen								

32C	1	1	1	1	1	1	1	1
Cursor X displacement from top left								

32D	3	3	3	3	3	3	3	3
Cursor Y displacement from top left								

32E	136	144	160	136	200	208	200	121
LSB Cursor address								

32F	55	55	55	71	91	91	99	124
MSB Cursor address								

330	0	0	0	0	0	0	0	0
MSB Top right y-coord of graphics window								

331	108	108	108	108	108	108	108	108
LSB Top right y-coord of graphics window								

332	1	0	0	0	0	0	0	0
MSB Graphics window top right x-coord								

333	10	133	66	66	133	66	33	66
LSB Graphics window top right x-coord								

334	0	0	0	0	0	0	0	0
MSB Graph. wind. bot. right y-coord								

335	12	12	12	12	12	12	12	12
LSB Graph. wind. bot. right y-coord								

336	0	0	0	0	0	0	0	0
MSB Graph. wind. bot. right. x-coord								

337	30	15	7	7	15	7	3	7
LSB Graph. wind. bot. right x-coord								

338	1	1	1	1	1	1	1	1
	MSB Y-coord of graphics origin							

339	234	234	234	234	234	234	234	234
	LSB Y-coord of graphics origin							

33A	1	1	1	1	1	1	1	1
	MSB X-coord of graphics origin							

33B	244	244	244	244	244	244	244	244
	LSB X-coord of graphics origin							

33C	1	1	1	0	1	1	0	0
	MSB Current y-coord graphics cursor							

33D	165	165	165	50	165	165	50	50
	LSB Current y-coord graphics cursor							

33E	0	0	0	0	0	0	0	0
	MSB Current x-coord graphics cursor							

33F	234	234	234	60	234	234	60	60
	LSB Current x-coord graphics cursor							

340	0	0	0	0	0	0	0	0

341	227	227	227	135	227	227	135	135

342	1	0	0	0	0	0	0	0

343	111	183	91	70	183	91	35	70

344	1	1	1	1	1	1	1	1

345	234	234	234	234	234	234	234	234
346	1	1	1	1	1	1	1	1
347	244	244	244	244	244	244	244	244
348	4	4	4	4	4	4	4	4
349	12	12	12	12	12	12	12	12
34A	0	0	0	0	0	0	0	0
34B	30	15	7	7	15	7	3	7
34C	4	4	4	4	4	4	4	4
34D	0	0	0	0	0	0	0	0
34E	86	86	86	86	86	86	86	86
34F	0	0	0	0	0	0	0	0
350	61	30	15	15	30	15	15	15
351	254	254	254	254	254	254	254	254
352	130	130	130	130	130	130	130	130

353	254	254	254	254	254	254	254	254
354	40	40	40	40	40	40	40	40
355	0	0	0	0	0	0	0	0
356	0	0	0	0	0	0	0	0
357	0	0	0	0	0	0	0	0
358	0	0	0	0	0	0	0	0
359	0	0	0	0	0	0	0	0
35A	0	0	0	0	0	0	0	0
35B	0	0	0	0	0	0	0	0
35C	0	0	0	0	0	0	0	0
35D	0	0	0	0	0	0	0	0
35E	0	0	0	0	0	0	0	0
35F	0	0	0	0	0	0	0	0
360	0	0	0	0	0	0	0	0

Addr								
1361	0	0	0	0	0	0	0	0
1362	0	0	0	0	0	0	0	0
1363	141	141	141	141	141	141	141	141
1364	218	218	218	218	218	218	218	218
1365	0	0	0	0	0	0	0	0
1366	0	0	0	0	0	0	0	0
1367 Current screen mode	0	1	2	3	4	5	6	7
1368	0	0	0	1	2	2	3	4
1369	136	16	32	136	136	16	136	17
136A	0	1	2	0	0	1	0	0
136B See text	8	8	8	8	8	8	8	8
136C	255	255	15	255	255	255	255	255
136D CLS/scroll filler byte	0	240	12	0	0	240	0	32
136E Graphics foreground mask	0	0	48	0	0	0	0	255

36F	255	15	51	255	255	15	255	0
Graphics background mask								
370	1	1	1	1	1	1	1	0
Graphics foreground modifier								
371	4	4	4	4	4	4	4	0
Graphics background modifier								
372	196	196	196	196	196	196	196	196
373	201	201	201	201	201	201	201	201
374	103	103	103	103	103	103	103	114
375	1	3	15	1	1	3	1	0
Colours available								
376	8	16	32	8	8	16	8	1
Bytes per character								
377	7	3	1	0	7	3	0	0
Pixels per byte								
378	0	0	0	0	0	0	0	0
379	128	136	170	128	128	136	128	128
37A	1	17	85	1	1	17	1	1
37B	0	0	0	0	0	0	0	0

| 37C | 48 | 48 | 48 | 48 | 48 | 48 | 48 | 48 |

| 37D | 27 | 27 | 27 | 27 | 27 | 27 | 27 | 27 |

| 37E | 13 | 13 | 13 | 13 | 13 | 13 | 13 | 13 |
Edit mode

| 37F | 127 | 127 | 127 | 127 | 127 | 127 | 127 | 127 |

| 380 | 127 | 127 | 127 | 127 | 127 | 127 | 127 | 127 |

| 381 | 197 | 197 | 197 | 197 | 197 | 197 | 197 | 197 |

| 382 | 15 | 15 | 15 | 15 | 15 | 15 | 15 | 15 |
See text

| 383 | 21 | 21 | 21 | 21 | 21 | 21 | 21 | 21 |

| 384 | 20 | 20 | 20 | 20 | 20 | 20 | 20 | 20 |

| 385 | 19 | 19 | 19 | 19 | 19 | 19 | 19 | 19 |

| 386 | 18 | 18 | 18 | 18 | 18 | 18 | 18 | 18 |

| 387 | 17 | 17 | 17 | 17 | 17 | 17 | 17 | 17 |

| 388 | 16 | 16 | 16 | 16 | 16 | 16 | 16 | 16 |

| 389 | 12 | 12 | 12 | 12 | 12 | 12 | 12 | 12 |

38A	0	0	0	0	0	0	0	0
Start of pallette								
38B	7	1	1	7	7	1	7	7
38C	3	3	2	2	2	3	3	3
38D	7	7	3	3	3	7	7	7
38E	4	4	4	4	4	4	4	4
38F	5	5	5	5	5	5	5	5
390	6	6	6	6	6	6	6	6
391	7	7	7	7	7	7	7	7
392	8	8	8	8	8	8	8	8
393	9	9	9	9	9	9	9	9
394	10	10	10	10	10	10	10	10
395	11	11	11	11	11	11	11	11
396	12	12	12	12	12	12	12	12
397	13	13	13	13	13	13	13	13

398	14	14	14	14	14	14	14	14
399	15	15	15	15	15	15	15	15
End of pallette								
39A	255	255	255	255	255	255	255	255
39B	255	255	255	255	255	255	255	255
39C	255	255	255	255	255	255	255	255
39D	255	255	255	255	255	255	255	255
39E	255	255	255	255	255	255	255	255
39F	255	255	255	255	255	255	255	255
3A0	45	45	45	45	45	45	45	45
Start of printer buffer								
3A1	45	45	45	45	45	45	45	45
3A2	45	45	45	45	45	45	45	45
3A3	45	45	45	45	45	45	45	45
3A4	45	45	45	45	45	45	45	45
3A5	45	45	45	45	45	45	45	45

3A6	45	45	45	45	45	45	45	45
3A7	45	45	45	45	45	45	45	45
3A8	45	45	45	45	45	45	45	45
3A9	13	13	13	13	13	13	13	13
3AA	124	124	124	124	124	124	124	124
3AB	51	51	51	51	51	51	51	51
3AC	48	48	48	48	48	48	48	48
3AD	51	51	51	51	51	51	51	51
3AE	32	32	32	32	32	32	32	32
3AF	124	124	124	124	124	124	124	124
3B0	32	32	32	32	32	32	32	32
3B1	50	50	50	50	50	50	50	50
3B2	53	53	53	53	53	53	53	53
3B3	53	53	53	53	53	53	53	53

|3B4		32	32	32	32	32	32	32	32	
|3B5		50	50	50	50	50	50	50	50	
|3B6		53	53	53	53	53	53	53	53	
|3B7		53	53	53	53	53	53	53	53	
|3B8		32	32	32	32	32	32	32	32	
|3B9		50	50	50	50	50	50	50	50	
|3BA		53	53	53	53	53	53	53	53	
|3BB		53	53	53	53	53	53	53	53	
|3BC		32	32	32	32	32	32	32	32	
|3BD		50	50	50	50	50	50	50	50	
|3BE		53	53	53	53	53	53	53	53	
|3BF		53	53	53	53	53	53	53	53	
|3C0		13	13	13	13	13	13	13	13	
|3C1		45	45	45	45	45	45	45	45	

```
|3C2 |   45   45   45   45   45   45   45   45 |
|                                              |
------------------------------------------------
|3C3 |   45   45   45   45   45   45   45   45 |
|                                              |
------------------------------------------------
|3C4 |   45   45   45   45   45   45   45   45 |
|                                              |
------------------------------------------------
|3C5 |   45   45   45   45   45   45   45   45 |
|                                              |
------------------------------------------------
|3C6 |   45   45   45   45   45   45   45   45 |
|                                              |
------------------------------------------------
|3C7 |   45   45   45   45   45   45   45   45 |
|                                              |
------------------------------------------------
|3C8 |   45   45   45   45   45   45   45   45 |
|                                              |
------------------------------------------------
|3C9 |   45   45   45   45   45   45   45   45 |
|                                              |
------------------------------------------------
|3CA |   45   45   45   45   45   45   45   45 |
|                                              |
------------------------------------------------
|3CB |   45   45   45   45   45   45   45   45 |
|                                              |
------------------------------------------------
|3CC |   45   45   45   45   45   45   45   45 |
|                                              |
------------------------------------------------
|3CD |   45   45   45   45   45   45   45   45 |
|                                              |
------------------------------------------------
|3CE |   45   45   45   45   45   45   45   45 |
|                                              |
------------------------------------------------
|3CF |   45   45   45   45   45   45   45   45 |
|                                              |
```

```
-----------------------------------------------------
|3D0 |   45    45    45    45    45    45    45    45 |
|                                                     |
-----------------------------------------------------
|3D1 |   45    45    45    45    45    45    45    45 |
|                                                     |
-----------------------------------------------------
|3D2 |   45    45    45    45    45    45    45    45 |
|                                                     |
-----------------------------------------------------
|3D3 |   45    45    45    45    45    45    45    45 |
|                                                     |
-----------------------------------------------------
|3D4 |   45    45    45    45    45    45    45    45 |
|                                                     |
-----------------------------------------------------
|3D5 |   45    45    45    45    45    45    45    45 |
|                                                     |
-----------------------------------------------------
|3D6 |   45    45    45    45    45    45    45    45 |
|                                                     |
-----------------------------------------------------
|3D7 |   45    45    45    45    45    45    45    45 |
|                                                     |
-----------------------------------------------------
|3D8 |   45    45    45    45    45    45    45    45 |
|                                                     |
-----------------------------------------------------
|3D9 |   45    45    45    45    45    45    45    45 |
|                                                     |
-----------------------------------------------------
|3DA |   45    45    45    45    45    45    45    45 |
|                                                     |
-----------------------------------------------------
|3DB |   45    45    45    45    45    45    45    45 |
|                                                     |
-----------------------------------------------------
|3DC |   45    45    45    45    45    45    45    45 |
|                                                     |
-----------------------------------------------------
```

```
|3DD |   45   45   45   45   45   45   45   45 |
|    |                                         |
----------------------------------------------
|3DE |   45   45   45   45   45   45   45   45 |
|    |                                         |
----------------------------------------------
|3DF |   45   45   45   45   45   45   45   45 |
|    | End of printer buffer                   |
----------------------------------------------
|3E0 |  135  135  135  135  135  135  135  135 |
|    | Start of run time keyboard buffer       |
----------------------------------------------
|3E1 |  135  135  135  135  135  135  135  135 |
|    |                                         |
----------------------------------------------
|3E2 |  135  135  135  135  135  135  135  135 |
|    |                                         |
----------------------------------------------
|3E3 |  135  135  135  135  135  135  135  135 |
|    |                                         |
----------------------------------------------
|3E4 |  135  135  135  135  135  135  135  135 |
|    |                                         |
----------------------------------------------
|3E5 |  135  135  135  135  135  135  135  135 |
|    |                                         |
----------------------------------------------
|3E6 |  135  135  135  135  135  135  135  135 |
|    |                                         |
----------------------------------------------
|3E7 |  135  135  135  135  135  135  135  135 |
|    |                                         |
----------------------------------------------
|3E8 |  135  135  135  135  135  135  135  135 |
|    |                                         |
----------------------------------------------
|3E9 |   13   13   13   13   13   13   13   13 |
|    |                                         |
----------------------------------------------
|3EA |   82   82   82   82   82   82   82   82 |
|    |                                         |
----------------------------------------------
```

3EB	85	85	85	85	85	85	85	85
3EC	78	78	78	78	78	78	78	78
3ED	13	13	13	13	13	13	13	13
3EE	135	135	135	135	135	135	135	135
3EF	135	135	135	135	135	135	135	135
3F0	127	127	127	127	127	127	127	127
3F1	127	127	127	127	127	127	127	127
3F2	51	51	51	51	51	51	51	51
3F3	57	57	57	57	57	57	57	57
3F4	135	135	135	135	135	135	135	135
3F5	135	135	135	135	135	135	135	135
3F6	135	135	135	135	135	135	135	135
3F7	135	135	135	135	135	135	135	135
3F8	135	135	135	135	135	135	135	135

```
|3F9 | 135 135 135 135 135 135 135 135 |
|                                      |
 --------------------------------------
|3FA | 135 135 135 135 135 135 135 135 |
|                                      |
 --------------------------------------
|3FB | 135 135 135 135 135 135 135 135 |
|                                      |
 --------------------------------------
|3FC | 135 135 135 135 135 135 135 135 |
|                                      |
 --------------------------------------
|3FD | 135 135 135 135 135 135 135 135 |
|                                      |
 --------------------------------------
|3FE | 135 135 135 135 135 135 135 135 |
|                                      |
 --------------------------------------
|3FF | 135 135 135 135 135 135 135 135 |
|   End of run time keyboard buffer    |
 --------------------------------------
```

Section three: BASIC program storage

The format in which BASIC programs are stored is as follows:

PAGE	&D—'return'
PAGE+1	MSB of line number
PAGE+2	LSB of line number
PAGE+3	Length of line
....	Text of line
PAGE+N	&D—'return'
PAGE+N+1	MSB of line number
PAGE+N+2	LSB of line number
PAGE+N+3	Length of line
PAGE+N+4	Start of text of next line
etc...	

Each line of text is preceded by the sequence 'return'/line number/length of line. The end of the program is indicated by a line number whose first byte is &FF.

The text of the lines is stored in normal ASCII codes, except for a few special cases:

— All keywords are stored as tokens. These are single byte abbreviations.

—The line numbers in GOSUB/GOTO/RESTORE/ON...GOTO/ON...GOSUB are stored in special binary format.

The tokens used are listed in the User Guide. A point to watch is that certain keywords are not totally tokenised. For example, TOP is tokenised as the keyword 'TO', as in FOR, followed by the ASCII letter 'P'.

The format used following a GOTO or GOSUB is particularly involved:
The line number is replaced by a byte 141, followed by three bytes of code:

Bits —	7	6	5	4	3	2	1	0
Byte 1	0	1	128s	64s	0	16384s	0	0
Byte 2	0	1	32s	16s	8s	4s	2s	1s
Byte 3	0	1	8192s	4096s	2048s	1024s	512s	256s

to represent the line number.

Those bits with a bar across their values are one if the line number does not contain the value, and zero if it does. The format is thus basically binary, except that the order of the bits has been altered.

As an example, the line GOTO 12345 will be 'hand tokenised':
the code of GOTO is &E5, so this will be the first byte of the line.
A space follows, so the next byte is &20.
Then we get the code 141, or &8D (oddly enough, the double
height code in teletext graphics).

The number 12345 in binary is "0011000000111001".

This can be better expressed as:

1 unit
0 twos
0 fours
1 eight
1 sixteen
1 thirty-two
0 sixty-fours
0 one-hundred-and-twenty-eights
0 two-hundred-and-fifty-sixes
0 five-hundred-and-twelves
0 one-thousand-and-twenty-fours
0 two-thousand-and-forty-eights
1 four-thousand-and-ninety-six
1 eight-thousand-and-one-hundred-and-ninety-two
0 sixteen-thousand-three-hundred-and-eighty-fours

Thus the binary format for the next three bytes is as follows:

Byte 1	0	1	0	1	0	1	0	0
Byte 2	0	1	1	1	1	0	0	1
Byte 3	0	1	1	1	0	0	0	0

In hexadecimal, this is:

Byte 1	&54
Byte 2	&79
Byte 3	&70

To check this, try this program. I have included a printout sample
run to reassure you!

```
   10 GOTO 12345
12345 FOR T%=PAGE TO PAGE+20
12346 PRINT ^T%,^?T%
12347 NEXT T%
 RUN
        E00        D
        E01        0
```

103

E02	A
E03	B
E04	20
E05	E5
E06	20
E07	8D
E08	54
E09	79
E0A	70
E0B	D
E0C	30
E0D	39
E0E	12
E0F	20
E10	E3
E11	20
E12	54
E13	25
E14	3D

The bytes I have described start at &E05.

The idea of using this peculiar code is to increase the speed of various operations concerning statements like GOTO/GOSUB/ RESTORE/ON...GOTO. The most obvious advantage of this approach is that GOTO 1 occupies the same space as GOTO 32767. Thus, the command RENUMBER need only alter these three bytes, and the two bytes containing each line number to renumber the whole program. Actually, it renumbers the lines, and then looks for any byte 141s. When it finds one, the three bytes following it are renumbered. On other computers, the whole program text may need to be moved about, to accommodate the differing lengths of program lines as the GOTO and GOSUB destinations are altered.

The other advantage occurs when the line is being interpreted — the computer need not convert a string of ASCII digits into binary before acting on the command — it has them in a form of binary already.

It should be noted that the only part of this of use to a good programmer is the RESTORE statements option when it is included with a line number.

There is a table starting at address &806D in the BASIC ROM which contains all the keywords in ASCII, followed by their tokens. The table ends at address &8358.

The format of the table is: ASCII Characters/token/spare byte and so on. The end of the ASCII characters is gauged by when the next character is greater than 127, since all tokens are &80 or greater. The spare byte is used to show certain things about the keyword, which need not concern us here.

The program which follows prints out all legal keywords and their tokens, by accessing the table. I have included a sample run:

```
  10 VDU 14
  20 T%=&806D
  30 REPEAT
  40 REPEAT
  50 PRINT CHR$(?T%);
  60 T%=T%+1
  70 UNTIL ?T%>127
  80 PRINT STRING$(20-POS,".");~?T%
  90 T%=T%+2
 100 UNTIL T%>=&8358
 110 VDU 15
RUN
AND...................80
AES...................94
ACS...................95
ADVAL.................96
ASC...................97
ASN...................98
ATN...................99
AUTO..................C6
BGET..................9A
BPUT..................D5
COLOUR................FB
CALL..................D6
CHAIN.................D7
CHR$..................BD
CLEAR.................D8
CLOSE.................D9
CLG...................DA
CLS...................DB
COS...................9B
COUNT.................9C
DATA..................DC
```

```
DEG.................9D
DEF.................DD
DELETE..............C7
DIV.................81
DIM.................DE
DRAW................DF
ENDPROC.............E1
END.................E0
ENVELOPE............E2
ELSE................8B
EVAL................A0
ERL.................9E
ERROR...............85
EOF.................C5
EOR.................82
ERR.................9F
EXP.................A1
EXT.................A2
FOR.................E3
FALSE...............A3
FN..................A4
GOTO................E5
GET$................BE
GET.................A5
GOSUB...............E4
GCOL................E6
HIMEM...............93
INPUT...............E8
IF..................E7
INKEY$..............BF
INKEY...............A6
INT.................A8
INSTR(..............A7
LIST................C9
LINE................86
LOAD................C8
LOMEM...............92
LOCAL...............EA
LEFT$(..............C0
LEN.................A9
LET.................E9
LOG.................AB
```

```
LN....................AA
MID$(.................C1
MODE..................EB
MOD...................83
MOVE..................EC
NEXT..................ED
NEW...................CA
NOT...................AC
OLD...................CB
ON....................EE
OFF...................87
OR....................84
OPENIN................AD
OPENOUT...............AE
PRINT.................F1
PAGE..................90
PTR...................8F
PI....................AF
PLOT..................F0
POINT(................B0
PROC..................F2
POS...................B1
RETURN................F8
REPEAT................F5
REPORT................F6
READ..................F3
REM...................F4
RUN...................F9
RAD...................B2
RESTORE...............F7
RIGHT$(...............C2
RND...................B3
RENUMBER..............CC
STEP..................88
SAVE..................CD
SGN...................B4
SIN...................B5
SQR...................B6
SPC...................89
STR$..................C3
STRING$(..............C4
```

```
SOUND................D4
STOP.................FA
TAN..................B7
THEN.................8C
TO...................B8
TAB(.................8A
TRACE................FC
TIME.................91
TRUE.................B9
UNTIL................FD
USR..................BA
VDU..................EF
VAL..................BB
VPOS.................BC
WIDTH................FE
PAGE.................D0
PTR..................CF
TIME.................D1
LOMEM................D2
HIMEM................D3
```

Notice how only those functions which take two or more arguments include the bracket in the token. This is because arguments taking a single argument may have the brackets ommitted. At the end of the table, the pseudo variables appear again. Their tokens here are used when the variable appears on the right-hand side of an assignment statement. You can see how this works in the list of keywords in the manual.

On the subject of pseudo variables, here is a list of the locations where TOP, HIMEM, PAGE, and LOMEM can be found:

Name	LSB	MSB
TOP	&12	&13
PAGE		&1D
HIMEM	&6	&7
LOMEM	&0	&1

Knowing these locations should only be useful to the machine language programmer, since BASIC programmers are already provided with the tools to alter and interrogate these locations.

If you ever need to alter a BASIC program from within a BASIC program, I would be inclined to add the changes to the keyboard buffer, using programs given in the last section, rather than using the indirection operators. If you do do this, remember that BASIC will accept lines of input which are still tokenised.

Section four: BASIC variables storage

This chapter is intended to lead you through an exploration of the ways the BBC computer stores variables, arrays, functions and procedures.

In the last section, I gave the locations where TOP, PAGE, HIMEM and LOMEM are stored. There is one important location missing from that list, however, The User Guide tells us that variables are stored just above the text of the current program, and then grow upwards. Thus, there should be a pointer to the top of variables, or the next free location after the variables.

The first step in our exploration is thus to find where that pointer is stored. I reasoned that when no variables existed, the free space pointer should be the same as LOMEM. Thus, I used this program to find all the locations which contained the same number as LOMEM:

```
  10 FOR T%=&00 TO &FF
  20 IF (!T% AND &FFFF)=LOMEM THEN PRIN
T ^T%
  30 NEXT T%
  40 END
RUN
   0
   2
  12
  17
```

Then I declared a variable, to see which locations remained:

```
  5 ASD=234
RUN
   0
  12
PRINT (!2 AND &FFFF)
3786
PRINT (!17 AND &FFFF)
49407
PRINT LOMEM
3776
```

After running the program again, it became apparent that the free space pointer must be stored at either location 2, or location &17. So I tested the values in these two locations, and concluded that the free space pointer must be stored at address 2, since location 17 contained a number that was far too big.

The next step was to construct a program to list out the contents of memory between TOP and the free space pointer, since this is the area where variables are stored. The program I used was:

```
1000 @%=4
1010 FOR T%=TOP TO (!2 AND &FFFF)
1020 PRINT ^T%,^?T%;
1030 A%=?T% MOD 128
1040 IF A%>31 THEN PRINT "---->";CHR$(A%
);
1050 PRINT
1060 NEXT T%
```

(I should mention why I am continually using single character integer variables. As you know, these variables are not cleared by RUN or CLEAR. It turns out that they are stored in a special area of memory, from &400 to &46C. These addresses were found by looking at the lower portion of memory while defining some integer variables. Thus, as they are stored in a special area of memory, they do not affect the free space pointer. This is useful where, as in this case, we are looking at a few variables, and do not want to be confused with other variables. Another point to notice about the storage of the integer variables is that they are stored at fixed locations, and thus may be located very quickly. @% is stored first, followed by A% to Z%. A four byte binary format is used for storage).

The program prints out all addresses in hex, and the number stored there. If the contents of the location is not a control code, the ASCII representation is displayed too.

Having designed the program I had to give it a variable to work on:

```
10 LET A=23
   RUN
   E7F    17
   E80     0
   E81     0
   E82    85
```

```
E83    38---->8
E84     0
E85     0
E86     0
E87    3E---->>
```

110

As you can see from the sample run, the letter 'A' does not appear in the variable storage area. This was a little odd. I tried with a longer variable name:

```
10  LET  ASDFGHJKL=3.1415926535897
RUN
E94    D
E95    0
E96    53----->S
E97    44----->D
E98    46----->F
E99    47----->G
E9A    48----->H
E9B    4A----->J
E9C    4B----->K
E9D    4C----->L
E9E    0
E9F    82
EA0    49----->I
EA1    F
EA2    DA----->Z
EA3    A2----->"
EA4    17
```

Now you can see the entire name of the variable, except the first letter. You can also see the five byte floating point representation of PI starting at address &E9F. This format should be explained.

For this explanation, I quote from Toni Baker's 'Mastering machine code on your ZX81 or ZX80', published by Interface:

"Here is a list of the first few integers as five byte floating point numbers:

Decimal	Floating point representation				
0	00	00	00	00	00
1	81	00	00	00	00
2	82	00	00	00	00
3	82	40	00	00	00
4	83	00	00	00	00
5	83	20	00	00	00
6	83	40	00	00	00
7	83	60	00	00	00
8	84	00	00	00	00
9	84	10	00	00	00
10	84	20	00	00	00

"There is a kind of pattern, but it's not instantly recognisable. Take a look at the negative numbers:

Decimal	Floating point representation				
−1	81	80	00	00	00
−2	82	80	00	00	00
−3	82	C0	00	00	00
−4	83	80	00	00	00
−5	83	A0	00	00	00
−6	83	C0	00	00	00
−7	83	E0	00	00	00
−8	84	80	00	00	00

"As you can see, you can instantly change a number from positive to negative just by adding 80 to the second byte. This doesn't apply to zero by the way — zero is represented uniquely to help speed arithmetic a little.

"Knowing how the floating point representation is built up will slightly help your understanding of the arithmetic processes, so I will give here a brief explanation of how to turn decimal numbers into a floating point representation numbers. It only takes a few simple steps.

"STEP ONE: If the number is zero, then its floating point representation is 00 00 00 00 00.

"STEP TWO: Ignoring the sign of the number, write it in binary (but without any leading zeros). For example:

7	111
−10	1010
−4.25	100.01
0.325	0.011

"Notice that the binary form has a binary point, not a decimal point! 100.01 means one four plus no 2s plus no 1s (here we reach the binary point) plus no halves plus one quarter. The next column would have been an eighth.

"STEP THREE: Is to work out a quantity called the EXPONENT. This is done as follows: if the part of the number to the left of the binary point is *not zero* then the exponent is the number of digits to the left of the point. If the number to the left of the point is zero and the first digit after the decimal point is one, then the exponent is *zero*. If the part of the number to the number to the left of the point is zero and the first digit after the point is zero, then count the number of zeros to the right of the point up to the first 1 — the exponent is minus this number. The first byte is &80 plus the exponent.

Decimal	Binary	Exponent	First byte
7	111	3	83
-10	1010	4	84
-4.25	100.01	3	83
0.325	0.011	-1	7F

"STEP FOUR: Now we can ignore the point — that is what the exponent is for — to tell the computer where the point is supposed to be. So ignoring the point, write the binary form *starting with the first one* and then add sufficient zeros to the right to make the whole thing thirty two bits long.

7	1110 0000 0000 0000 0000 0000 0000 0000
-10	1010 0000 0000 0000 0000 0000 0000 0000
-4.25	1000 1000 0000 0000 0000 0000 0000 0000
0.325	1100 0000 0000 0000 0000 0000 0000 0000

"STEP FIVE: It is here that we consider the sign of the original number. If the sign was negative, then we do nothing. If it was positive then replace the first one by a zero. Thus:

7	0110 0000 0000 0000 0000 0000 0000 0000
-10	1010 0000 0000 0000 0000 0000 0000 0000
-4.25	1000 1000 0000 0000 0000 0000 0000 0000
0.325	0100 0000 0000 0000 0000 0000 0000 0000

"STEP SIX: Now just convert these numbers into hex, like so, remembering to add the exponent byte in at the start:

7	83 60 00 00 00
-10	84 A0 00 00 00
-4.25	83 88 00 00 00
0.325	7F 40 00 00 00

Going back to the printout of ASDFGHJKL, you can see that the name is terminated by a zero, which is followed by the five byte floating point representation of PI.

But where is the first letter of the name? And what are the first two bytes for? (The last byte, &17, is present because the free space pointer points to the next free location, and so the program includes the first free location in the printout.)

I reckoned that the first letter was stored somewhere else in memory, so I tried the following:

```
CLEAR
MODE 4
VDU 28,0,0,0,0
VDU 23,0,12,0;0;0;0;0;
LET ZXC=23
LET X=234
LET Y=234
LET A=235
LET fdghfg=23
```

If you look at the third line down the screen, towards the right, as you type in the assignment statements, you should see some alteration in the byte patterns appearing. Try CLEARing, and then creating variables starting with each letter of the alphabet. You should see an area changing from black to apparently random bytes, growing to the right. If you have a very clear TV you should see that each assignment adds two bytes to the list. The other thing to notice is that each letter of the alphabet (upper and lower case) has two locations dedicated to it. It turns out that the location assigned to A has address &482. One can then derive the formula (&400 + ASC(A$)*2) to give the address of the two bytes associated with the letter in A$.

Now return to mode 7, and try the following:

```
MODE 7
CLEAR
10 LET A=23
RUN
E7F    F1----->q
E80    0
E81    0
E82    85
E83    38----->8
E84    0
E85    0
E86    0
E87    20----->
PRINT ~(!&482 AND &FFFF)
E7F
```

Does the number &E7F, given in the contents of the locations assigned to the letter 'A', ring any bells? It's the first address used by the storage of the variable.

Thus, the computer keeps a table of two bytes per initial letter of each variable, starting at &482 for the letter 'A', and the address in this table

114

gives the start of the variable with this starting letter. Zero in this table means that no variable starts with that letter. But, what happens if two or more variables start with the same letter?

The only thing to do is to create another variable starting with the same letter, and see how it is stored:

```
20 LET AF=23
RUN
E8B    93
E8C    E
E8D    0
E8E    85
E8F    38----->8
E90    0
E91    0
E92    0
E93    FF--->
E94    0
E95    46---->F
E96    0
E97    85
E98    38---->8
E99    0
E9A    0
E9B    0
E9C    0
```

We can assume that the contents of locations &482 and &483 are &E8B. The storage of the first variable is the same as before, apart from some new values in the previously redundant initial two bytes. You may notice that the address in these two bytes is the start address of the block describing the second variable. So a useful new hypothesis would be that (in addition to the points outlined above), if the contents of the first two bytes of the block are less than 256, the current block is the last variable starting with that letter, and if the two bytes contain a number greater than 255, that the number is the address of the next variable with the same initial letter.

This arrangement is a great deal more powerful than that commonly employed in computers of this type. Most microcomputers employ a free space pointer, and just place each new variable onto the end of the list. Thus when the computer has to find the value of a variable, it has to search all the way through the list until it finds the one it wants. The BBC computer only has to search through those that share the same starting letter. You may like to see if you can get a speed reduction in the running of a program by making all the variables used start with different letters. It is possible to get a 10% reduction in speed by doing this. But, real variables are only a small part of the story. We have to investigate strings, muiti-character integer variables, and all the different types of array. We'll start with integer variables with long names.

I added these two lines to the original program, and obtained these results:

```
DELETE 10,20
10 LET AA%=23
20 LET AB%=24
RUN
E8E    97
E8F     E
E90    41---->A
E91    25---->%
E92     0
E93    17
E94     0
E95     0
E96     0
E97    85
E98     0
E99    42---->B
E9A    25---->%
E9B     0
E9C    18
E9D     0
E9E     0
E9F     0
EA0     0
PRINT ^(!&482 AND &FFFF)
E8E
```

The first point to notice is that not only is the name of the variable minus the first character stored, but the percentage sign is stored too. The sequence is, as before, terminated by a zero, preceding the four byte binary representation of the integer. These four bytes may be interrogated with the word indirection operator, (!).

You will also notice that the table is used in the same way as the real variables, and that the link bytes are used in the same way. We can now progress onto string variable storage. I added these two lines to the program, with the following results:

```
DELETE 10,20
10 LET AB$="JJ"
20 LET AC$="HH"
RUN
E92    9D
E93     E
E94    42----->B
E95    24----->$
E96     0
E97    9B
E98     E
E99     2
E9A     2
E9B    4A----->J
E9C    4A----->J
E9D     0
E9E     0
E9F    43----->C
EA0    24----->$
EA1     0
EA2    A6----->&
EA3     E
EA4     2
EA5     2
EA6    48----->H
EA7    48----->H
EA8     0
```

The two bytes at &E92 point to the next string variable, seeing though they both begin with 'A', so the linking appears to be the same as used in integer and real variables. The next two bytes are, again, the name of the variable, minus the first letter, which is stored in the table at &482. Next comes the zero, to mark the end of the name. The next two bytes form an address which points to the contents of the variable, in this case the two 'J's at &E9B. The two 2 s would appear to be the length of the string, but why is it there twice? The tree is again terminated by the two zero bytes for the address of the next variable starting with 'A'.

A little experiment was called for to see which of the two bytes (which apparently held the length of the string) were used by the LEN function.

```
PRINT LEN(AB$)
   2
?&E99=1
PRINT LEN(AB$)
   2
?&E9A=1
PRINT LEN(AB$)
   1
?&E99=12
PRINT LEN(AB$)
   1
```

The first thing I did was check that the length of the variable was indeed two, and as you can see, it was.

Next, I tried altering the byte in &E99, and printed the length of the string. It remained at two, indicating that the LEN function was not getting its data from the first byte of the two holding the length. The second byte was then altered, and the length printed. It had now changed, so I knew that the length of the string was stored in the second of the two bytes. (The section in The User Guide on CALL reveals that the first length byte gives the number of bytes allocated.)

Before going on to arrays, here is a short re-cap of the points so far mentioned. To store the value of a variable, the computer goes through the following steps:

STEP ONE: Take the ASCII code of the first letter of the name. Work out the address associated with it from the formula 'address = &400 + ascii__code*2'.

STEP TWO: Extract the address stored in that location.

STEP THREE: If the address is zero, store the value of the free space pointer in the location. Then go to step six.

STEP FOUR: Go to the address.

STEP FIVE: Go to step two.

STEP SIX: Place the block describing the variable starting at the address in the free space pointer, using zero for the first two bytes, since this is the last variable with that starting letter. Update the free space pointer with the next free location.

You may have to read through that a number times before it is clear. The blocks for each type of variable are:

REAL VARIABLES

- Two bytes, for the address of the next variable of any type with the same starting letter.
- Any remaining letters of the name, besides the first one.
- A zero byte.
- Five bytes for the value of the variable.

INTEGER VARIABLES

- Two bytes, for the address of the next variable with the same starting letter.
- Any remaining letters of the name, including the percentage sign.
- Zero byte.
- Four byte value of the variable.

STRING VARIABLES

● Two bytes, pointing to any other variables with the same initial letter.
● Any other letters of the name, including the $ sign.
● A zero byte.
● Two bytes, containing the address of the contents of the variable.
● The number of bytes allocated to the string.
● Length of string.
● String data.

But, looking back at the printout, what happens if we adjust AB$ to have three letters in it? There isn't room to put the three letters in place of the two 'J's. So let's see what happens:

```
30 LET AB$="123"
RUN
EA2   AD---->-
EA3    E
EA4   42---->B
EA5   24---->$
EA6    0
EA7   B8---->8
EA8    E
EA9    3
EAA    3
EAB   4A---->J
EAC   4A---->J
EAD    0
EAE    0
EAF   43---->C
EB0   24---->$
EB1    0
EB2   B6---->6
EB3    E
EB4    2
EB5    2
EB6   48---->H
EB7   48---->H
EB8   31---->1
EB9   32---->2
EBA   33---->3
EBB   66---->f
```

As you can see, the new value of AB$ has been placed at the top of the variable area, with the two 'J's now being redundant. The two address bytes have been updated to cope with the contents of the variable moving around.

Having done that, let's see what happens if a string is made to have different contents of the same length, or a shorter length.

```
40 LET AB$="#$%"
RUN
EB2    BD---->=
EB3    E
EB4    42---->B
EB5    24---->$
EB6    0
EB7    C8---->H
EB8    E
EB9    3
EBA    3
EBB    4A---->J
EBC    4A---->J
EBD    0
EBE    0
EBF    43---->C
EC0    24---->$
EC1    0
EC2    C6---->F
EC3    E
EC4    2
EC5    2
EC6    48---->H
EC7    48---->H
EC8    23---->#
EC9    24---->$
ECA    25---->%
ECB    0
```

As you can see, the previous contents are overwritten.

A conclusion to be drawn from this is that if you make all string variables as long as you are ever likely to need right at the start of each program using the function STRING$, you will find the computer never needs to find extra storage space for its contents as it increases. This is equivalent to dimensioning strings on other computers.

ARRAYS

Now we can look at arrays. I started by looking at a single dimension string array.

```
DELETE 10,40
10 DIM A$(2)
10 DIM ASDF$(2)
RUN
E83   F1---->q
E84    0
E85   53---->S
E86   44---->D
E87   46---->F
E88   24---->$
E89   28---->(
E8A    0
E8B    3
E8C    3
E8D    0
E8E    0
E8F    0
E90    0
E91    0
E92    0
E93    0
E94    0
E95    0
E96    0
E97    0
E98    0
E99    0
E9A   24---->$
```

The first two bytes are, as we would expect, pointers to the next variable starting with the letter 'A'.

Then we get the rest of the letters of the name, including the dollar symbol and the opening bracket of the array.

The zero byte signifies the end of the sequence.

The rest of the sequence is hard to work out, so I filled up the array, and then re-ran the program. (I unfortunately forgot the name of the array in mid-type, as the printout testifies!)

```
 20 LET A$(0)="A"
 30 LET A$(1)="B"
 40 LET A$(2)="C"


LIST,999
  10 DIM ASDF$(2)
  20 LET A$(0)="A"
  30 LET A$(1)="B"
  40 LET A$(2)="C"
  20 LET ASDF$(0)="A"
  30 LET ASDF$(1)="B"
  40 LET ASDF$(2)="C"
REM WHOOPS !
RUN
EBC    4
EBD    0
EBE   53--->S
EBF   44--->D
EC0   46--->F
EC1   24--->$
EC2   28--->(
EC3    0
EC4    3
EC5    3
EC6    0
EC7   D3--->S
EC8    E
EC9    1
ECA    1
ECB   D4--->T
ECC    E
ECD    1
ECE    1
ECF   D5--->U
ED0    E
ED1    1
ED2    1
ED3   41--->A
ED4   42--->B
ED5   43--->C
ED6    0
```

The two threes are the number of elements of the array. There does not, however, appear to be any indicator of the number of dimensions.

Next comes three blocks containing the address of each element, and its length, again written twice. It is safe to assume that the second length indicator is the one used by the LEN function, and the first is the number of bytes allocated.

The next step was to look at a real array.

```
DELETE 10,40
10 DIM ASD(2)
20 LET ASD(0)=PI
30 LET ASD(1)=PI
40 LET ASD(2)=P
40 LET ASD(2)=PI
RUN
EAE    1A
EAF     0
EB0    53----->S
EB1    44----->D
EB2    28----->(
EB3     0
EB4     3
EB5     3
EB6     0
EB7    82
EB8    49----->I
EB9     F
EBA    DA----->Z
EBB    A2----->"
EBC    82
EBD    49----->I
EBE     F
EBF    DA----->Z
EC0    A2----->"
EC1    82
EC2    49--->I
EC3     F
EC4    DA--->Z
EC5    A2--->"
EC6     0
```

The format would appear to be similar to the string array, except that the five bytes describing each element appear instead of the blocks of address and length data about each element. The data starts at address &EB7 in the example.

There still is no noticeable way of telling the number of dimensions.

I next turned to integer, two dimensional arrays.

```
DELETE 10,40
10 DIM ASD%(1,1)
20 ASD%(0,0)=123
30 ASD%(0,1)=&7FFFFFFF
40 ASD%(1,0)=1
50 ASD%(1,1)=&01020304
RUN
ED6    1A
ED7     0
ED8    53---->S
ED9    44---->D
EDA    25---->%
EDB    28---->(
EDC     0
EDD     5
EDE     2
EDF     0
EE0     2
EE1     0
EE2    7B---->{
EE3     0
EE4     0
EE5     0
EE6    FF---->
EE7    FF---->
EE8    FF---->
EE9    7F---->
EEA     1
EEB     0
EEC     0
EED     0
EEE     4
EEF     3
EF0     2
EF1     1
EF2     0
```

The general format appears familiar, except the block between the data and the zero byte indicating the end of the name. What has previously been a three, has changed to a five. After some experimentation I concluded that this byte contains $2*n+1$, where n is the number of dimensions of the array. This holds true for any type of array. The next four bytes are the number of elements in each of the two dimensions. Then we get the familiar four byte data for each element.

The program I used to test my hypothesis about the $2*n+1$ formula was this one:

```
DELETE 10,50
10 DIM KJ%(1,1,1,1)
RUN
E87   3B---->;
E88    0
E89   4A---->J
E8A   25---->%
E8B   28---->(
E8C    0
E8D    9
E8E    2
E8F    0
E90    2
E91    0
E92    2
E93    0
E94    2
E95    0
E96    0
E97    0
E98    0
E99    0
E9A    0
E9B    0
E9C    0
E9D    0
E9E    0
E9F    0
EA0    0
EC9    0
ECA    0
```

```
ECB    0
ECC    0
ECD    0
ECE    0
ECF    0
ED0    0
ED1    0
ED2    0
ED3    0
ED4    0
ED5    0
ED6    1A
```

As you can see, for reasons of space conservation, I have left out a large chunk in the middle of the printout.

The array has four dimensions, and the byte is 9, which measures up nicely with the formula.

While musing on the speed of the BBC Computer I ran the following series of experiments.

```
  10  GOTO 100
  20  DEF PROCHELLO
  30  PRINT "HELLO"
  40  ENDPROC
 100  PROCHELLO
RUN
HELLO
 200  PROCHELLO
```

The program above calls a procedure to print the word 'HELLO' twice.

The next step was to find the address of the word 'HELLO' in line 20.

```
FOR T%=PAGE TO PAGE+19:P. ?T%,T%:N.
          13          3584
           0          3585
          10          3586
          11          3587
          32          3588
         229          3589
          32          3590
```

128

```
   141        3591
    68        3592
   100        3593
    64        3594
    13        3595
     0        3596
    20        3597
    13        3598
    32        3599
   221        3600
    32        3601
   242        3602
    72        3603
PRINT ASC("H")
    72
PRINT ^3603
E13
```

Given that the ASCII code for 'H' is 72, the start of the word is address 3603, or &E13.

To test this, I placed the code for 'A' into the start of the word, and printed out the program:

```
?&E13=65
LIST
   10 GOTO 100
   20 DEF PROCAELLO
   30 PRINT "HELLO"
   40 ENDPROC
  100 PROCHELLO
  200 PROCHELLO
?&E13=72
101 ?&E13=65
RUN
HELLO
HELLO
```

The 'A' was then replaced with an 'H'.

A line was inserted between the two calls to the procedure, to change the 'H' to an 'A'. The program ran perfectly, even though at the second call, PROCHELLO did not exist!!

Listing the program confirmed this:

```
  10 GOTO 100
  20 DEF PROCAELLO
  30 PRINT "HELLO"
  40 ENDPROC
 100 PROCHELLO
 101 ?&E13=65
 200 PROCHELLO
?&E13=72
LIST
  10 GOTO 100
  20 DEF PROCHELLO
  30 PRINT "HELLO"
  40 ENDPROC
 100 PROCHELLO
 101 ?&E13=65
 200 PROCHELLO
```

The next step was to replace the 'A' again with an 'H'.

There are many conclusions that can be drawn from the above points. The first is that after the first call has been made to a procedure, the name of the procedure in the DEF statement does not matter. Thus the computer is storing the address of PROCHELLO, together with its name in some place in its memory. It was a safe bet that this area was the variable storage area, so after I had dissected the variable storage, discussed earlier, I started to explore the storage of procedures, and functions, presuming that the function mechanism is the same as the procedure mechanism.

I used the program I presented before to list out the variable area, but added a procedure definition:

```
2000 DEF PROCHELLO
2010 PRINT "HELLO"
2020 ENDPROC
```

```
  10 PROCHELLO
1070 END
  LIST
    10 PROCHELLO
  1000 @%=4
  1010 FOR T%=TOP TO (!2 AND &FFFF)
  1020 PRINT ^T%,^?T%;
  1030 A%=?T% MOD 128
  1040 IF A%>31 THEN PRINT "--->";CHR$(A%
);
  1050 PRINT
  1060 NEXT T%
  1070 END
  2000 DEF PROCHELLO
  2010 PRINT "HELLO"
  2020 ENDPROC
  RUN
HELLO
  EA6    29--->)
  EA7     0
  EA8    48--->H
  EA9    45--->E
  EAA    4C--->L
  EAB    4C--->L
  EAC    4F--->O
  EAD     0
  EAE    90
  EAF     E
  EB0     0
```

When the program is run, the variable list area surprisingly holds the whole name of the procedure, starting at &EA8. Perhaps the initial letter table is not used for procedures?

However, the initial two bytes of the block are still there, so some form of linking is employed in the storage of procedures. The procedure name is terminated by a zero byte.

Then we get what appears to be a 16 bit address. &E90 will probably be the address of the first byte of the procedure. Judicious use of the indirection operator will confirm this.

Using the same methods as outlined previously, examining the starting pages of memory while calling procedures, it turns out that procedures have a dedicated address in the table at &482. The relevant address is &4F6. If you check, you will find that after the program has been run, the address contained is &EA6.

```
PROCHELLO
HELLO
 PRINT ~(!&4F6 AND &FFFF)
 EA6
```

Next, I checked to see if functions were organised in the same way:

```
DELETE 2000,2020
10 PRINT FNHELLO
2000 DEF FNHELLO="HELLO"
RUN
HELLO
 E9C   20---->
 E9D    0
 E9E   48---->H
 E9F   45---->E
 EA0   4C---->L
 EA1   4C---->L
 EA2   4F---->O
 EA3    0
 EA4   92
 EA5    E
 EA6   29---->)
PRINT ~(!&4F8 AND &FFFF)
 E9C
```

As you can see, things are similar. It turns out that location &4F8 is used as the function pointer. To recap, functions and procedures are linked together via their first two bytes, and the address &4F6 and &4F8. The block contains the name and the start address of the function/procedure. After doing all this, the final program looked like this:

```
  10 PRINT FNHELLO
1000 @%=4.
1010 FOR T%=TOP TO (!2 AND &FFFF)
1020 PRINT ^T%,^?T%;
1030 A%=?T% MOD 128
1040 IF A%>31 THEN PRINT "--->";CHR$(A%
);
1050 PRINT
1060 NEXT T%
1070 END
2000 DEF FNHELLO="HELLO"
```

Using some of the information contained in this chapter, here is an
application program to list out all the variables which are active when it
is run.

```
  10 REM Copright (C) Jeremy Ruston
  20 REM eg :
  30 ZXC%=234
  40 H=23.345
  50 GFHJTRJ_SEG=PI
  60 ASD$="A STRING"
  70 D$="ANOTHER"
  80 DIM R(10)
  90 DIM RF(3,4)
 100 DIM A%(23)
 110 DIM WER%(1,3,2)
 120 DIM K$(23)
 130 DIM HJE$(2,4,1)
1000 REM ****************************
1010 REM Variable list...
1020 REM Lists integer, real and
1030 REM string variables.
1035 REM (1777 bytes long !)
```

```
1040  REM *********************************
1050  @%=0
1060  DIM E% 255
1070  FOR T%=&482 TO &4F4 STEP 2
1080  IF FNDD(T%)<>0 THEN PROCfollow(FND
D(T%),(T%-&400)/2)
1090  NEXT T%
1100  END
1110  REM *********************************
1120  DEF PROCfollow(T%,S%)
1130  $E%=CHR$(S%)
1140  R%=T%+1
1150  PRINT CHR$(S%);
1160  REPEAT
1170  R%=R%+1
1180  IF ?R%>64 THEN PRINT CHR$(?R%);:$E
%=$E%+CHR$(?R%)
1190  UNTIL ?R%<64
1200  IF ?R%=&25 THEN PROCinteger
1210  IF ?R%=&24 THEN PROCstring
1220  IF ?R%=&00 THEN PROCreal
1230  IF ?R%=&28 THEN PROCreal_array
1240  IF FNDD(T%)>255 THEN PROCfollow(FN
DD(T%),S%)
1250  ENDPROC
1260  REM *********************************
1270  DEF PROCinteger
1280  IF R%?1=0 THEN PRINT "%=";EVAL($E%
+"%"):ENDPROC
1290  PRINT "%(";
1300  FOR D%=1 TO ((R%?3)-1)/2
1310  IF D%<>1 THEN PRINT ",";
1320  PRINT FNDD(D%*2+R%+2)-1;
1330  NEXT D%
1340  PRINT ")"
1350  ENDPROC
1360  REM *********************************
1370  DEF PROCstring
1380  IF R%?1=0 THEN PROCnormal_string E
LSE PROCstring_array
1390  ENDPROC
```

```
1400 REM ******************************
1410 DEF PROCnormal_string
1420 PRINT "$=";
1430 PRINT CHR$(34);
1440 IF R%?5=0 THEN PRINT CHR$(34):ENDP
ROC
1450 FOR L%=1 TO R%?5
1460 PRINT CHR$(?(L%-1+FNDD(R%+2)));
1470 NEXT L%
1480 PRINT CHR$(34)
1490 ENDPROC
1500 REM ******************************
1510 DEF PROCstring_array
1520 PRINT "$(";
1530 FOR D%=1 TO ((R%?3)-1)/2
1540 IF D%<>1 THEN PRINT ",";
1550 PRINT FNDD(D%*2+R%+2)-1;
1560 NEXT D%
1570 PRINT ")"
1580 ENDPROC
1590 REM ******************************
1600 DEF PROCreal
1610 PRINT "=";EVAL($E%)
1620 ENDPROC
1630 REM ******************************
1640 DEF PROCreal_array
1650 PRINT "(";
1660 FOR D%=1 TO ((R%?2)-1)/2
1670 IF D%<>1 THEN PRINT ",";
1680 PRINT FNDD(D%*2+R%+1)-1;
1690 NEXT D%
1700 PRINT ")"
1710 ENDPROC
1720 REM ******************************
1730 DEF FNDD(A%)=!A% AND &FFFF
RUN
ASD$="A STRING"
A%(23)
D$="ANOTHER"
GFHJTRJ_SEG=3.14159265
H=23.345
```

```
HJE$(2,4,1)
K$(23)
R(10)
RF(3,4)
WERZ(1,3,2)
ZXCZ=234
```

The idea was for a routine which could be placed in an unused section of memory and then called whenever a record of variables contents was required during program development.

The program as presented here uses a set of dummy variables, lines 30 to 130 as a demonstration. To use the program, you would omit these lines, and situate it near the top of memory. Then, when you have run the program from which you wish to dump variables, return PAGE to the variable list program, and type RUN. Remember the CTRL-B if you want printer output.

If you RUN the program as it stands, you should notice a number of things about its output.

First, the variables are printed in alphabetical order of first letters. This may give you an idea of how the program operates.

Second, in the case of arrays, the computer just prints out the dimensions of the array, rather than wasting space with its contents.

Because the program must not upset any of the variables used by the original program, it uses integer variables throughout. This also means that the single string used must be created rather deviously.

1050 Sets the field width to zero. This is because of the need for the array dimensions to be printed next to each other.
1060 This line dimensions the string used in the program. It allows for variable names up to 255 characters long in this version. You may like to restrict the length to 30 or so!
1070 Starts a loop through all of the initial variable name letters in that table.
1080 If any variables exist starting with that letter, call PROCFOLLOW, which will follow the tree and print out the variables as it comes across them.
1090 Ends the loop through all the letters.
1100 Ends the program.
1120 Starts the definition of PROCFOLLOW. This procedure is called with the address of where it can find a variable, and the initial letter of the variable. It will carry on calling itself

recursively until this address is less than 256, which indicates the end of the tree.

1130 $E% will hold the name of the variable, so it is started off with the letter PROCFOLLOW was called with.

1140 R% is used to point to the next letter of the name in the list. It is set to the second link byte here, to allow for variables which are only a single character long.

1150 PRINTS the first letter of the name.

1160 Starts a REPEAT loop, which will continue until all the letters of the name have been printed.

1170 Increments R%, to point to the next letter. You can now see why R% was first set to be a 'byte too low'.

1180 If the next letter is a legal one, prints it, and adds the letter to $E%.

1190 Ends the loop when an invalid letter came up.

1200 This line starts a section of code which calls various procedures, depending on the nature of the variable being processed. If the next character in the name was a percentage sign, for example, this line sends the program off to the integer variable handling procedure.

1210 If it was a dollar sign, the string procedure is called.

1220 If the next byte was the zero byte, there is no modifier on the end of the variable name, so it must be a real variable, so the REAL procedure is called.

1230 If the next character was a bracket, there is no symbol between the end of the name and the bracket, so it must be a real array.

1240 If the link bytes for this variable are legal, recursively calls PROCFOLLOW to follow the link bytes.

1250 Or else, end the procedure. If this procedure has been called a number of times all the ENDPROCs will fall through each other, so neatly ending the whole program.

1270 Starts the definition of PROCINTEGER. This procedure processes integer variables and integer arrays.

1280 If the next byte after the percentage sign is zero, it is not an array, so prints out its contents, using EVAL in a way never intended by its designers, and exists.

1290 Otherwise, it must be an array, so print the opening bracket.

1300 Starts a loop through all the dimensions of the array. The last parameter of the FOR statement is a derivation of the $2*n+1$ formula.

1310 If this is not the first dimension, prints the separating comma.

1320 Prints the number of elements in the current dimension.

1330 Ends the loop.

1340 Prints the closing bracket.

1350 Ends PROCINTEGER.

1370 Starts the definition of PROCSTRING.

1380 If it is an array, call PROCSTRING__ARRAY, else call PROCNORMAL__STRING. The test is made by seeing if there is an opening bracket in the name of the variable.

1390 Ends PROCSTRING.

1410 Starts the definition of PROCNORMAL__STRING.

1420 Prints the equals sign, and subscripts the variable.

1430 Prints the opening quote of the contents of the string.

1440 If the string is null, prints the closing quote, and returns.

1450 For each of the characters in the string,

1460 Prints the character,

1470 Ends the loop.

1480 Prints the closing quote.

1490 Ends PROCNORMAL__STRING.

1510 Starts the definition of PROCSTRING__ARRAY.

1520 Prints the subscript and the opening bracket of the array.

1530 Starts a loop through all of the dimensions of the string array.

1540 If this is not the first dimension, prints the separating comma.

1550 Prints the number of elements in the current dimension.

1560 Ends the loop.

1570 Prints the closing bracket of the array.

1580 Ends PROCSTRING__ARRAY

1600 Starts the definition of PROCREAL.

1610 Prints the equals sign, and the value of the variable.

1620 Ends PROCREAL.

1640 Starts the definition of PROCREAL__ARRAY.

1650 This section of code is almost identical to that in lines 1520 to 1570

1730 Defines a double byte interrogation function.

For easy reference, this table lists the locations of all the single letter integer variables:

```
@% is stored at &400
A% is stored at &404
B% is stored at &408
C% is stored at &40C
D% is stored at &410
E% is stored at &414
F% is stored at &418
G% is stored at &41C
H% is stored at &420
I% is stored at &424
J% is stored at &428
K% is stored at &42C
L% is stored at &430
M% is stored at &434
N% is stored at &438
O% is stored at &43C
P% is stored at &440
Q% is stored at &444
R% is stored at &448
S% is stored at &44C
T% is stored at &450
U% is stored at &454
V% is stored at &458
W% is stored at &45C
X% is stored at &460
Y% is stored at &464
Z% is stored at &468
```

And similarly, here is a table of locations for the first letter of other variables:

'A'--->	&482	'K'--->	&496
'B'--->	&484	'L'--->	&498
'C'--->	&486	'M'--->	&49A
'D'--->	&488	'N'--->	&49C
'E'--->	&48A	'O'--->	&49E
'F'--->	&48C	'P'--->	&4A0
'G'--->	&48E	'Q'--->	&4A2
'H'--->	&490	'R'--->	&4A4
'I'--->	&492	'S'--->	&4A6
'J'--->	&494	'T'--->	&4A8

```
'U'--->    &4AA          'h'--->    &4D0
'V'--->    &4AC          'i'--->    &4D2
'W'--->    &4AE          'j'--->    &4D4
'X'--->    &4B0          'k'--->    &4D6
'Y'--->    &4B2          'l'--->    &4D8
'Z'--->    &4B4          'm'--->    &4DA
'['--->    &4B6          'n'--->    &4DC
'\'--->    &4B8          'o'--->    &4DE
']'--->    &4BA          'p'--->    &4E0
'^'--->    &4BC          'q'--->    &4E2
'_'--->    &4BE          'r'--->    &4E4
'`'--->    &4C0          's'--->    &4E6
'a'--->    &4C2          't'--->    &4E8
'b'--->    &4C4          'u'--->    &4EA
'c'--->    &4C6          'v'--->    &4EC
'd'--->    &4C8          'w'--->    &4EE
'e'--->    &4CA          'x'--->    &4F0
'f'--->    &4CC          'y'--->    &4F2
'g'--->    &4CE          'z'--->    &4F4
```

This program is not the most useful you'll find in this book:

```
10  REM ??????????????????????
20  LET A=PI
30  FOR T%=&484 TO &4F4 STEP 2
40  ?T%=?&482
50  T%?1=?&483
60  NEXT T%
RUN
PRINT Q
3.14159265
PRINT W
3.14159265
PRINT R
3.14159265
PRINT JK
3.14159265
PRINT I
3.14159265
PRINT P
3.14159265
```

```
PRINT B
3.14159265
PRINT M
3.14159265
PRINT V
3.14159265
PRINT X
3.14159265
PRINT F
3.14159265
PRINT H
3.14159265
PRINT Y
3.14159265
PRINT HII
No such variable
REM Etc, etc...
```

It creates a variable 'A' and then directs all the other variable pointers to the same variable. The net effect is that every variable you later create will be treated as if it started with the letter 'A'. This is demonstrated after the listing by printing a whole lot of single character variables, and amazingly, they are all the same as 'A'!

Can you think of any more useful applications for having two routes or more to a single variable?

I thought not, but later I was faced with passing an array to a procedure (the same technique is applicable to user definable functions). The solution I came up with is demonstrated in this program:

```
 10 REM *******************************
 20 REM Passing arrays to procedures.
 30 REM Copyright (C) Jeremy Ruston
 40 REM *******************************
 50 DIM N$(2),M$(2)
 60 N$(1)="LED"
 70 N$(2)="ZEPPELIN"
 80 M$(1)="ARE"
 90 M$(2)="GREAT"
100 PROCexample("N$")
```

```
 110 PROCexample("M$")
 120 END
 130 REM ********************************
1000 DEF FNfind(A$)
1010 LOCAL B$,ad,add,first
1020 first=ASC(A$)
1030 ad=!(first*2+&400) AND &FFFF
1040 REPEAT
1050 IF ad<255 THEN PRINT '"No such arr
ay at PROCfind":END
1060 add=ad
1070 B$=""
1080 REPEAT
1090 ad=ad+1
1100 B$=B$+CHR$(ad?1)
1110 UNTIL ad?1=0
1120 ad=!add AND &FFFF
1130 UNTIL B$=MID$(A$,2)+"("+CHR$(0)
1140 =add
1150 REM ********************************
2000 DEF PROCexample(array_name$)
2010 LOCAL
2020 add=FNfind(array_name$)
2030 ?&4BE=add MOD 256
2040 ?&4BF=add DIV 256
2050 FOR T=1 TO 2
2060 PRINT _$(T)
2070 NEXT T
2080 ENDPROC
2090 REM ********************************
RUN
LED
ZEPPELIN
ARE
GREAT
```

The only general part of the program is PROCfind(A$). This procedure finds the address of the first link byte of the array of name A$. A$ should not contain the opening bracket of the name, but it should contain the modifier ($ or %).

PROCfind is based on some of the routines in the variable list program, so it should not need a detailed explanation.

The routine is based on the assumption that you will not have any arrays in your program called '_' (underscore). If you do, the array will be lost.

Having entered PROCfind, all you have to do to include an array in the parameters of your functions or procedures is:

i) Everywhere you want to have an array as a parameter, use a suitably named string — as in line 2000 of the example program.

ii) Then use PROCfind to work out the start address of the array of this name (line 2020).

iii) Then substitute this address for the pointer for a character not often used to start variable names, such as the underscore character.

iv) Then use the underscore character, or whatever you chose, as the name of the array you used as the parameter. Remember to put the correct modifiers after it.

If more than one array has to be passed, I would be inclined to use different names for them, such as 'p', 'q', 'r' and 's'.

This program is a derivation of the movement program I gave in chapter one.

If you have the movement program on cassette, it would be quicker to modify that than to type this whole program in.

```
10 REM Copyright (C) Jeremy Ruston
20 REM MCMLXXXII
30 MODE 1
40 VDU 19,3,4,0,0,0
50 VDU 5
60 PROCASSEMBLE
70 START%=HIMEM/8
80 X%=0
90 Y%=0
100 B%=20
110 A%=1
120 REPEAT
130 B%=B%-1
```

```
  140 IF B%=0 THEN B%=RND(20)+10:A%=RND(
64)-1:GCOL 0,RND(3)
  150 IF A% AND 1 THEN Y%=(Y%+31) MOD 32
  160 IF A% AND 2 THEN Y%=(Y%+1) MOD 32
  170 IF A% AND 4 THEN X%=(X%+1) MOD 80
  180 IF A% AND 8 THEN X%=(X%+79) MOD 80
  190 IF A% AND 16 THEN X%=(X%+1) MOD 80
  200 IF A% AND 32 THEN X%=(X%+79) MOD 8
0
  210 S%=START%+X%+Y%*80
  220 ?&D00=S% DIV 256
  230 ?&D01=S% MOD 256
  240 CALL &D10
  250 R%=S%*8
  260 ?&322=R% MOD 256
  270 ?&323=R% DIV 256
  280 VDU 30,42
  290 UNTIL FALSE
  300 DEF PROCASSEMBLE
  310 P%=&D10
  320[OPT 0
  330 LDA #12:STA &FE00
  340 LDA &D00:STA &FE01
  350 LDA #13:STA &FE00
  360 LDA &D01:STA &FE01
  370 RTS:]
  380 ENDPROC
```

OS 1.0

Since this book was written, a new operating system for the BBC Microcomputer
has been issued. This sheet describes
the differences between the old operating system and the current version.

To find out what version of the operating system you have, type *FX 0. If
the computer prints 'OS EPROM 0.10' you
have the old operating system. The
current operating system is identified
by the message 'OS 1.X'. If you find
you have a series 1 operating system,
read the book in conjunction with this
sheet.

Section One
No change.

Section Two
The current operating system stores much
the same information as the old, except
it uses different locations:

(All addresses are in hex)

300 - LSB X-coordinate of bottom right
of graphics window.
301 - MSB X-coordinate of bottom right
of graphics window.
302 - LSB Y-coordinate of bottom right
of graphics window.
303 - MSB Y-coordinate of bottom right
of graphics window.
304 - LSB X-coordinate of top left of
graphics window.

305 - MSB X-coordinate of top left of graphics window.
306 - LSB Y-coordinate of top left of graphics window.
307 - MSB Y-coordinate of top left of graphics window.

308 - X-coordinate of bottom left of text window.
309 - Y-coordinate of bottom left of text window.
30A - X-coordinate of top right of text window.
30B - Y-coordinate of top right of text window.

30C - LSB X-coordinate of origin.
30D - MSB X-coordinate of origin.
30E - LSB Y-coordinate of origin.
30F - MSB Y-coordinate of origin.

318 - Cursor X position.
319 - Cursor Y position.

34A - LSB text cursor address.
34B - MSB text cursor address.

34E - MSB screen memory start address. (LSB is not stored, but assumed to be zero.)
34F - Bytes per character.
350 - LSB address of top left of screen.
351 - MSB address of top left of screen.
352 - LSB bytes per line.
353 - MSB bytes per line.
354 - Screen memory length.
355 - MODE.

358 - CLS/scroll filler byte.
359 - Graphics foreground mask.
35A - Graphics background mask.

35B - Graphics foreground modifier.
35C - Graphics background modifier.

36Ø - Number of colours available.
361 - Number of pixels per byte.

36F to 37E - Pallette.

All these locations behave in the way described in the text.

Section Three
No change.

Section Four
No change.